The COUNTRY HOUSES of DAVID ADLER

INTERIORS BY FRANCES ELKINS

WITH A CATALOGUE RAISONNÉ OF HIS WORK

The COUNTRY HOUSES *of* DAVID ADLER

STEPHEN M. SALNY

Introduction by Franz Schulze

W. W. NORTON & COMPANY

New York • London

*Page 1: David Adler's signature printed with
the permission of the American Academy of Arts
and Letters, New York City.*

Frontispiece: Reception gallery, Clark house

For information about permission to reproduce selections from
this book, write to Permissions, W. W. Norton & Company, Inc.,
500 Fifth Avenue, New York, NY 10110

The text of this book is composed in Bembo
with the display set in Bembo
Manufacturing by Friesens
Book design by Abigail Sturges
Production Manager: Leeann Graham

Library of Congress Cataloging-in-Publication Data

Salny, Stephen M.
The country houses of David Adler / Stephen M. Salny; intro-
duction by Franz Schulze.
          p. cm.
Includes bibliographical references and index.
          ISBN 0-393-73045-X
1. Adler, David, 1882–1949—Criticism and interpretation. 2.
Country homes—Illinois—Chicago. I. Title.

NA737.A3 S25 2001
728'.092—dc21
00-069947

W. W. Norton & Company, Inc.,
500 Fifth Avenue, New York, N.Y. 10110
www.wwnorton.com

W. W. Norton & Company Ltd.,
10 Coptic Street, London WC1A 1PU

0 9 8 7 6 5 4 3 2

This book is dedicated to

J. DUDLEY CLENDINEN

*with gratitude for his loving support
and encouragement of everything I do*

CONTENTS

David Adler   *Frances Elkins*

INTRODUCTION

by Franz Schulze

In its attentions to the architects who were David Adler's contemporaries, the literature has customarily given pride of place to those figures who substantially changed the direction of the profession. Among the names that come most readily to mind in this connection, Le Corbusier, Mies van der Rohe, and Walter Gropius are remembered for turning decisively away from the uses of the past and, in the process, creating major new stylistic categories and theoretical approaches.

Adler, born like them in the 1880s, followed a notably different path. While he was a master of a variety of idioms, his work almost invariably took its cue from forms and references fixed in history. To some extent his choices were an outgrowth of the values of the world of his upbringing, where a society of wealth was dominated by people with conservative tastes. Nonetheless, his career stemmed in large part from his own personal decisions, which were consistently in harmony with his talents. That combination of preference and ability led to a body of work, as Stephen Salny persuasively argues, worthy of a high rank and a special place in the history of American building. Indeed, Salny's text is evidence of a lately renewed interest in residential architecture all in all separate from the modernist outlook. During the last several decades major studies by such scholars as James Ackerman, Liisa and Donald Sclare, Vincent Scully, Dell Upton, and Richard Guy Wilson have drawn attention, variously, to the Shingle style and the Stick style, the Arts and Crafts movement, classical revivals and assorted versions of the vernacular, and moreover to specific building types like villas, country houses, and estates. These categories were until lately seldom associated with "advanced" approaches in design, as they were formerly known.

Gradually, then, we have found ourselves more aware than ever of two histories, running on parallel tracks. One is the record of the aforementioned modernist movement, the other, that of an architecture palpably more historicist in motivation and representation.

The moves made by the modernists and their predecessors of the late nineteenth and early twentieth century were largely traceable to the shifts in technological and economic conditions that transformed western society. Cities mushroomed in size, redefined by the growth of railroads, the invention of the automobile, the appearance of huge factories and commercial structures, and the development of the metal-framed skyscraper. The story of modern building cannot be written without attention to Gustave Eiffel in France, Peter Behrens in Germany, the Chicago School of the 1880s, 1890s, and 1900s, including Louis Sullivan and Frank Lloyd Wright, and numerous anonymous contributions to the machine age aesthetic. What emerged was a number of new types of construction for which the old stylistic languages had little vocabulary and less syntax. No architectural manner popular during previous centuries would have been sufficient to give expression to the look of Eiffel's tower or the roadways hung from steel cables that are the chief identifying features of suspension bridges.

But much of the money generated by an industrialized society was in the hands of people whose own wishes for private residences indicative of their station followed from a conservative point of view. Architects of talent and ambition were attracted to such wealthy clients, so that the very period associated with the vanguardist innovators produced another company of designers, who invested the older styles with creative meaning of a different kind. Moreover, both constituencies profited from developments in transportation and communication at the end of the nineteenth century. Trains and transatlantic steamers moving at higher speeds enabled Americans to look with their own eyes on the historic monuments of Europe, and, of course, to draw inspiration from them. Added to this circumstance was an increasingly sophisticated printing technology, which yielded books containing vast amounts of information and imagery.

The best of the traditionalist architects associated with this period proved to be anything but copyists. Henry Hobson Richardson, by consensus one of the greatest American architects, is remembered for the profitable recasting of several manners that he had learned from direct contact with the past. "Richardsonian Romanesque," a term applied to round-arched, heavily rusticated buildings that Richardson based upon medieval antecedents but imbued with his own personality, manifestly suggests a combination of eclecticism and originality.

Richardson also helped to transform the Queen Anne, identified with earlier nineteenth-century British houses, into the Shingle style. The result was a uniquely American mode that was employed mostly in residences, to some degree in nostalgic emulation of vernacular usages of America's colonial past. The Shingle style's widespread popularity during the 1880s is due in part to the merits of the many able architects who practiced it, in the East, notably Bruce Price, Peabody & Stearns, Wilson Eyre, John Calvin Stevens, and McKim, Mead & White, and in the Chicago area, Henry Ives Cobb and Charles Frost.

In turn, no designer drew more attention to himself in the 1890s than Richard Morris Hunt, who designed some of the most palatial houses in America, the most spectacular of them commissioned by the Vanderbilt family. Greatly indebted to what he had learned as the first American to attend France's Ecole des Beaux-Arts, Hunt went on to champion the French academic point of view in his work and to become a major player in American society architecture at the turn of the twentieth century.

Thus, by the time David Adler was a college student (1900–1904), he could look back to a generation of residential building that drew richly upon a reserve of newly transformed stylistic approaches. His interest in the profession took wing at Princeton, leading him to design his earliest work while he was still an undergraduate. Thereafter, taking advantage of the possibilities of travel, Adler was able to see firsthand much of Europe, where he assembled a collection of postcards (now in Stephen Salny's hands) that provides a view of the buildings, many of them of chateaux in Normandy, that seem to have meant the most to him.

The tours of study at the Polytechnikum in Munich and especially at the Ecole des Beaux-Arts in Paris functioned as both cause and effect of his outlook as it developed in his early adult years. Following instruction in an atelier from Gustave Umbdenstock, a Paris architect, Adler gained admission to the Ecole in 1908 and remained there until 1911, a crucial span for an American, given the conditions that obtained during that time. Central to the effect of two major cultural phenomena of the nineteenth century, the Industrial Revolution and the Romantic movement, was the tendency to break or to depart from traditional systems and rules. Contrarily inclined, the Ecole, during its heyday in the late 1800s and early 1900s, sought to restore to architecture a respect for the best of balanced composition and historical form. Thus, despite its latter-day reputation for arch conservatism, the values of the Ecole can be regarded to a significant degree as reformist in intent. A measure of confirmation of that role as played out in the United States may be observed in the powerful impact of the Beaux-Arts esthetic on Chicago's World's Columbian Exposition of 1893. That event reflected the tastes of its supervising architect, Daniel Burnham, who maintained them a decade later in the classicist character that marked the plan and the buildings proposed by the historic 1909

Burnham-Bennett Plan of Chicago. By the time Adler returned to America in 1911, the stripped-down frame of the Chicago commercial school had already seen its best days, while Burnham's Beaux-Arts outlook enjoyed a position front and center.

In view of these circumstances, it makes sense that Adler would choose to work in a manner reflective of what he had learned in Paris and what he encountered in Chicago. It was there, after all, that he was hired by Howard Van Doren Shaw, a distinguished local architect who was at his most productive about the time the younger man joined his firm. Adler's first house, the C. A. Stonehill residence in Glencoe, Illinois, was designed while he was in Shaw's employ.

Both the time and the place were ready for Adler, and he for them. His earliest independently conceived houses materialized in the 1910s, after he had left Shaw's office, and they were done for a generation of Chicago clients both able and eager to utilize his special gift for eliciting elegance from historical form. The First World War had the effect of adding to the wealth of Chicago's society classes, who profited directly or indirectly from the city's prodigious industrial energy. With the turn of the 1920s families living in or near the Midwest's most socially upscale suburb, Lake Forest, began commissioning year-round estates meant to replace older homes that had earlier served for the summer season alone or were more and more perceived as old-fashioned. Adler and several other architects, chiefly Shaw, Delano & Aldrich, and Harrie Lindeberg, provided these clients with conservatively fashioned houses of ample size, to which opulent gardens were frequently added. While the Depression of the early 1930s was ruinous to the American econ-

omy, the well-to-do citizens of Lake Forest and nearby North Shore communities remained sufficiently prosperous to keep Adler busy with commissions well into the 1930s. Moreover, by that time his fame had spread far beyond Chicago. It is little wonder, then, that the period between the two World Wars proved to be his most fruitful. Moreover, during that span he steadfastly maintained his commitment to historicist form, utilizing it with masterful versatility.

It is also worth remembering that Adler's most active and successful period coincided with the time when the European modernist pioneers were working at the peak of their own powers, a conjunction evident from a comparison of the dates of several of his most memorable efforts with several of theirs. The Jesse Strauss residence in Glencoe, rendered in the manner of a French farmhouse, was completed in 1921, the same year as Erich Mendelsohn's expressionistic Einstein Tower in Potsdam. The Richard Crane house in Ipswich, Massachusetts, done in the Georgian style, was coeval with the epochal modernist housing colony, the Weissenhofsiedlung, erected in Stuttgart in 1927. The Tobin Clark house, executed in Tudor half-timber style, was built in 1930, when Le Corbusier's Villa Savoye was nearing completion in Poissy, France.

In the text that follows, Stephen Salny has provided a survey of the output of a singular artist, drawing attention to criteria that critical opinion at the dawning of the twenty-first century has come to regard with new respect. David Adler's residential buildings feature a unique blend of beauty and recognizability, values not commonly cited in the earlier textbooks but today more readily apparent than ever, to professionals and laymen alike.

Charter Club

Adler's sketch of Charter Club

AN OVERVIEW

David Adler's birth year of 1882 coincided with one of the most prolific periods of domestic architecture in the United States. Classical design, which had already taken root in this country, continued to flourish, especially under the leadership of Richard Morris Hunt (1827–1895), the first American to receive his architectural training at the Ecole des Beaux-Arts in Paris. Adler would eventually follow Hunt's path, including the disappointment of being denied entrance into this world-renowned institution on his first attempt—which, according to Beaux-Arts historian Richard Chafee, was not uncommon. In Adler's quest for eventual admission, he followed the prescribed procedure of joining an atelier in Paris, where he immersed himself in studying for the exam. On January 6, 1908, his diligence and determination were rewarded: he was accepted at the Ecole des Beaux-Arts.

Paris captured Adler's soul, but the Midwestern soil of Milwaukee, Wisconsin held his roots. Adler's paternal grandfather, David (1821–1905), had emigrated from Bohemia to the United States in 1846, eventually settling in Milwaukee where he went into the retail clothing business. By 1857 the business had become a flourishing wholesale concern, ranking the Adlers among the earliest successful Bohemian Jewish families to make a new life in the United States. Also involved in the business was David's son, Isaac David (1849–1925), the father of David Adler, Jr., the architect (1882–1949).

The Adler family's clothing business prospered into the third generation, though David Jr.'s involvement with his father's business was limited to the summer between his senior year at prep school—Lawrenceville—and his entrance to Princeton University. Adler's scholastic record was a mixed one. A letter of recommendation to Lawrenceville from the East Side High School in Milwaukee favorably described his two and a half years of classical and regular studies there. He was equally successful at Lawrenceville, where he focused on the classics in preparation for college. It was at Princeton that Adler's performance waned until his senior year, when his curriculum included several courses in architecture. Good marks in these courses, which involved the study and drawing of the classic orders, were not the sole indicators of his interest in architecture. In 1903, still an undergraduate, Adler designed the front elevation of the remodeled Charter Club, a Princeton University eating club to which he belonged. This first commission, which stemmed from his accomplished studies in architecture and seems to have confirmed his passion to himself, marked the beginning of an exemplary career. A classically symmetrical Georgian elevation, with portico entrance and dentilled cornice, it presaged the distinguished oeuvre that was to follow.

After graduating from Princeton in 1904, Adler's first stop along the way to becoming an architect was a course of study at the Polytechnikum in Munich, Germany, known for its

Postcard, Adler collection

teaching of industrial arts and applied sciences. By the winter of 1906, with three semesters of architectural training behind him, he set his sights on Paris and the Ecole des Beaux-Arts. There, Adler's younger sister, Frances (1888–1953), to whom he was extremely close, visited him. They traveled together through Europe, partaking of the architectural and botanical highlights, which Adler avidly documented. He collected five hundred picture postcards, to which he referred throughout his career, borrowing from them exact details for his own designs. They also met several avant-garde artisans, including Jean-Michel Frank (1895–1941), the French interior decorator and furniture designer, and Alberto Giacometti (1902–1985), the sculptor, who designed fixtures for Frank. Elkins would eventually promote both of them through the California-based interior decorating business that she established in 1918. In Europe brother and sister laid the foundation for their respective careers, not realizing the dynamic contributions they would make to architecture and design in the United States, both as collaborators and independently.

The curriculum at the Ecole encouraged Adler's innate design sensibilities. Symmetry, balance, and proportion, all attributes of his Charter Club façade, were important to the Beaux-Arts philosophy. Though lectures at the school covered numerous topics thoroughly, ranging from architectural history and theory to construction and building law, they served as only an adjunct to the most important part of

the education—the architectural *concours* or competitions by which students' designs were judged. Held monthly, the competitions emphasized the composition of either *esquisses* (sketches) or *projets rendus* (rendered projects). The prerequisites varied. The *esquisses* required students to draw a building in a twelve-hour period. The broader parameters of the *projets rendus* allotted about two months for the completion of three larger drawings of a more complex building. Also important to the curriculum were the construction *concours*, in which students produced a dozen drawings demonstrating their grasp of a building's assemblage. This represented the most difficult assignment of the "second class," and mastering it was required before a student could be promoted to the "first class." Despite the competency of Adler's other *concours*, because of his lack of interest in structural and technical applications, he chose not to take on this assignment. Instead, he returned to the United States, established himself in Chicago, and launched his architectural career.

Chicago proved to be the right choice for David Adler. Not only was it close to his family, but the city was also deeply rooted in Beaux-Arts precedents. One of its most influential architects, Daniel H. Burnham (1846–1912), had served as the chief architectural consultant for the Chicago World's Columbian Exposition of 1893. He emphasized the tenets of classical design, selecting for the project several East Coast architects of classical disposition, including Richard Morris Hunt and the firm of McKim, Mead & White, whose predominant whitewashed pavilions exemplified symmetry, order, and monumentality. This influence deeply affected a city that, before the Exposition, had been overlooked, even snubbed, by East Coast culture. Burnham's support of classical design did not deter the Chicago School, which, in fostering the advent of the skyscraper, eschewed historic references; it prospered well into the 1950s. But a wave of classicism was sweeping the country. By the time Adler returned to Chicago in 1911, the city was reorganizing—thanks to the Chicago Plan. Completed in 1909 under the auspices of Burnham and his colleague, architect Edward H. Bennett (1874–1954) for the Commercial Club, Chicago's leading group of businessmen, the plan utilized and expanded on the principles of balance and harmony that had characterized the Exposition architecture. The result was nothing less than the most important urban design in the United States. Like Paris, Chicago's city center became an efficient division of boulevards, landscaped parks, and waterfront promenades hosting an orderly sequence of classical buildings and civic institutions, all of which enhanced the city's economic viability.

Beaux-Arts classicism also contributed to the distinguished aura of Chicago's residential architecture. Richard Morris Hunt and H. H. Richardson (1838–1886) both designed houses there at the end of the century. While Adler, too, would augment the city with several notable buildings, it was on Chicago's North Shore, particularly in Lake Forest, that he forged his reputation as the preeminent designer of the country house.

Adler started out in the office of Howard Van Doren Shaw, a devotee of the Arts and Crafts movement. Shaw (1869–1926) was among the most prolific country-house architects on the North Shore. Although Shaw had commissions in Chicago and other parts of the country, the greatest concentration of his work was in Lake Forest, where, between the late 1890s and the middle 1920s, he designed over two dozen houses for the town's most promi-

nent families. Adler's prospective clientele would come from the same social circle.

Henry Dangler, Adler's closest friend from the Ecole and the person who introduced Adler to Katherine Keith, whom Adler married in 1916, also worked in Shaw's office. Adler and Dangler did not stay long with Shaw; they decided to form their own partnership. Dangler left first; Adler remained with Shaw only until he completed the design of his first house, which was for his uncle and benefactor Charles A. Stonehill, in the North Shore community of Glencoe.

The Adler-Dangler partnership resulted in the most productive period of Adler's thirty-eight-year career. In less than six years, it produced sixteen houses of English, French, and Italian derivation. Five were in Chicago and three in Lake Forest; it would be another decade before this community monopolized Adler's demanding schedule. Henry Dangler's death in 1917 left both a personal and professional void in Adler's life, for he had lost not only his partner but his best friend

Adler was not certified to practice architecture in Illinois. He obtained a New York license in 1917. Though Adler was the designer (Dangler had his own projects independent of Adler), the signature on the plans had always

Postcard, Adler collection

15

Postcards, Adler collection

been Dangler's. Adler was compelled to sit for the Illinois exam and, as presaged by his incomplete studies at the Ecole, he failed. Already on his way to becoming one of America's leading domestic architects, Adler now had to find another architect who could replace Dangler professionally. The solution came in another former associate from Shaw's office, Robert Work (1874–1960).

The association between David Adler and Robert Work was strictly one of convenience. According to Paul Schweikher (1903–1999), who worked as a draftsman in Adler's office between 1925 and 1927 and would later chair the Department of Architecture at Carnegie-Mellon University, Work was "really more a kind of employee . . . than a partner." Work and Adler's professional relationship, he added, was dissolved "as soon as Adler was equipped with a license of his own." That came in 1929, after Adler, with Work's name on the blueprints, had produced another sixteen houses. He obtained his New York license in 1917. Having practiced as a principal architect for ten years, he became eligible for the oral examination in Illinois. To date, Adler had designed over thirty houses and could also offer to the Illinois Architectural Commission the endorsements of several prominent architects and many gratified clients. New York architect Harrie T. Lindeberg (1879–1959), whose numerous Lake Forest commissions were contemporaneous with Adler's, attested to Adler's competency and character: "I am familiar with Mr. Adler's work and consider him one of the ablest architects in the country. His work in New York has been an inspiration to his fellow architects here. The fact that he has been intrusted with important work in the East is an indication of his integrity and ability." Lindeberg was referring to the fairly recent completion of an imposing Georgian townhouse in Manhattan for department-store heir Marshall Field III. Field himself praised Adler, gladly testifying in writing "as to his competency and faithfulness in the execution of the trust imposed." His association with Robert Work now dissolved, David Adler was ready to undertake work on his own.

Adler's professional achievement was marred by personal tragedy. In May 1930, his wife of fourteen years, Katherine Keith Adler (1893–1930), was killed in an automobile accident while she and Adler were motoring on a rain-slick road in Normandy. Katherine was driving, and the car skidded out of control and smashed into a tree. Adler sustained only minor physical injuries but was so distraught after her death that he was known to cry out her name in the night.

The Adlers did not have children, and Adler focused his devotion on his now divorced sister, Frances Elkins, their mother Theresa, and Frances's daughter Katherine. He moved Theresa into a house that he remodeled on his property in Libertyville, Illinois. Frances and Katherine lived in California, where Frances was already an established decorator, but Adler saw them often, especially as he and Frances reached their collaborative pinnacle during the 1930s. In fact, from 1919 until Adler's death in 1949, brother and sister worked on at least sixteen projects, including Frances's historic house, Casa Amesti, in Monterey.

Whatever the task, David Adler applied incomparable taste, ability, and standards. Katherine Elkins Boyd said that her uncle was "a purist" who was "without compromise in his work." Mrs. Boyd, herself an accomplished interior decorator like her mother, learned a great deal from her uncle. "One must go from room to room quietly," he told her, adding that there must always be "something off." Laurance Armour, Jr., recalled a similar sentiment: he heard Adler muse to his parents, Laurance and Lacy, as he planned the renovation of their Lake Forest house, "where could I make a mistake?"

Adler's job roster contains nearly three hundred entries Extensive renovations, like the Armour commission, represented a significant part of his work. Forty-five houses were built; at least another twenty never became a reality. Several commissions were halted because of the Depression, though many of Adler's clients were fortunately immune to its effects. (Lake Forest client Phoebe Bentley, whose South-African-Dutch colonial was built in 1928, recalled that she and her husband Richard had been especially lucky. In anticipation of building their house, they had liquidated their investments prior to the Crash, thus preserving their construction budget.)

The late 1920s through the middle 1930s were the culmination of Adler's career. His masterpiece—the Elizabethan half-timbered house

Postcards, Adler collection

of Celia Tobin Clark in Hillsborough, California—marked the start of this period. The commission was followed by the Pennsylvania Dutch–style Georgian for Helen Shedd Reed—unquestionably Adler's finest house on the North Shore. He built eight houses during this period, predominantly Georgian in style; the Clark house, a French manor farmhouse, and a Greek revival house were the three deviations.

The final phase of Adler's career was preceded, in 1935, by a riding accident at the Mill Creek Hunt Club, a club frequented by Adler's social circle, in Lake Villa, north of Lake Forest. Adler's involvement with Mill Creek was also a professional one; after the club relocated from a neighboring farm during the late 1920s, he was hired to design its replacement as well as new stables and a kennel. The end result—a quadrangular grouping of three white clapboard buildings—was a great success. Adler's riding ability, however, was not on par with his design abilities. He had taken up riding to please Katherine, relying on his docile horse, Firwood, to keep him safe and steady. Unfortunately, Firwood was not available on this particular day, and the fall that Adler suffered left him hospitalized for several weeks.

At the time of the accident, which occurred in the depths of the Depression, Adler was not working on any major commissions. His house for Lolita Armour in Lake Forest had recently been completed, and he was planning a

River House duplex in New York for Evelyn Marshall Field, among other additions and renovations. Not until the late 1930s was Adler again called upon to design houses, two of which were built in 1938—one for his brother- and sister-in-law Frederick and Elizabeth Keith and the other for North Shore residents Louis and Jane Kuppenheimer. Adler nicknamed the Kuppenheimer house, a whitewashed brick building of French and Georgian derivation, the "Bungalow," though it was not his smallest house. The Keiths' house, a one-story cottage built on Lido Key in Sarasota, Florida, more aptly fit this description.

After completing plans for the British Columbia retreat of John and Mickey Kellogg in 1939, Adler received one of the most creative remodeling projects of his career: the conversion of an abandoned post office building into an art museum in Santa Barbara, California. Santa Barbara was not new to Adler. One of his earliest houses, an Italian Renaissance villa, was built in Montecito, where he also redesigned a library for longtime Chicago friends and clients, Joseph and Annie Ryerson. It was at the suggestion of another Chicago friend, Katherine McCormick, that Adler received the museum commission. As a winter resident of Santa Barbara, Katherine McCormick was very active in museum affairs. The Italianate design appealed to him (nine of his houses had been

Postcard, Adler collection

built in this style). Central to Adler's plan for the new museum was the simplification of its entrance: he eliminated several bays of windows and the accompanying grille work and trim, so the arcaded entrance became the focal point of the façade. The interior, formerly the post office workroom, was divided into three spaces that became the exhibition gallery, the anteroom for a new gallery, and the service area.

In 1941, Adler was named a fellow of the American Institute of Architects. By then, however, what Adler loved passionately was no longer in vogue. By 1945, when the American Academy of Arts and Letters in New York, an organization that recognizes accomplishments in literature, music, and the fine arts, honored him, he wrote to architect Thomas Harlan Ellett, a 1943 Arts and Letters recipient who had proposed him, that the period of the "great house" was over and he was attempting to adapt to "very different work." Adler's 1948 commission for Paul and Ruth Winslow in Pebble Beach, California—his last house—exemplified his ability to create grandeur and elegance on a much smaller scale.

In the middle to late 1940s Adler sought a site for a vacation home for himself. First he chose Taxco, Mexico, where he planned to restore the Hacienda del Chorrillo. Taxco, one of his sister's favorite destinations, had once been the silver center of Mexico and the mountainside hacienda, which was an abandoned Spanish silver smelting factory dating back to the 1500s, held great promise as a second home. Adler's ambitious attempt to convert the structure was foiled by his intolerance of the inferior workmanship of the local crews.

Next he turned to a wooded twelve-acre parcel in Jack's Peak, near Carmel, California. Jack's Peak was close to Frances and their mutual friends in Pebble Beach. First, Adler designed the property's main house, a gabled colonial pavilion flanked by two wings. The symmetrical clapboard house would not be large, but its detailing, which included flat keystoned arches atop the first-floor windows and doorways, reflected Adler's usual refinement and exactitude. Balanced pairs of pedestaled urns and recessed busts would front the entrance façade, the busts echoing the detailing from Adler's Libertyville farmhouse. In the plans for the back of the house, where a terrace cantilevered out beyond the three windows of the living

Mrs. Katherine Adler

room and dining room, Adler whimsically specified stuffed moose heads to be mounted above each of the windows. Jack's Peak was to include a small white clapboard gardener's cottage, conceived one year after the main house. The cottage was the only building to be realized, for Adler died unexpectedly of a heart attack shortly thereafter, at the age of sixty-seven.

His death also halted two other commissions. One was for Mary Runnells, who had recently purchased a stately Prairie School house, designed by the Chicago architectural firm of Spencer & Powers (1905) in Lake Forest, and wanted Adler to oversee the alterations. He had done a splendid job twenty years earlier for Mary Runnells's sister, Lacy Armour. Adler's plans for the Runnells house, which were sitting on his desk when he died, except for the library mantel and bookshelves, were not executed. Boston architect George W. W. Brewster, son-in-law of Mary Runnells's good friends Donald and Isabel Ryerson, was engaged to make the alterations.

Another commission came from Joseph and Annie Ryerson. During the early 1920s he had designed for them a Louis XVI–style townhouse in Chicago, a classically elegant building

· NAME ·	· DESCRIPTION ·		PAGE ·	· BOX ·	TUBE ·
ADLER, D.	APT. 11 EAST ELM ST.		93	~~50~~	-
ADLER, D.	LIBERTYVILLE, ILL.		93	18	-
ADLER, D.	1240 Nº STATE ST.		93	50	-
ADLER, DAVID (OFFICE)	220 S. MICHIGAN AVE		187	~~50~~	-
ADLER, I.D.	MILWAUKEE, WIS.		95	#	-
ADLER, MRS. I.D.	LIBERTYVILLE, ILL.		221	85	-
ALLERTON, ROB'T	MONTICELLO, ILL.		223	#	-
ANDERSON, MRS. N.P.	FORT WORTH, TEXAS		117	##	5
ARMOUR, A.W.	LAKE FOREST, ILL.		145	21	NAME
ARMOUR, A.W.	209 LAKE SHORE DRIVE		145	21	-
ARMOUR, LAURENCE			-	55	-
ARMOUR, LAURANCE	APT. 1500 LAKE SHORE DRIVE		185	81	38
ARMOUR, LAURANCE	STABLES, LAKE FOREST, ILL.		186	79	38
ARMOUR, LAURANCE	ALTERATIONS & ADDITIONS TO HOUSE, LAKE FOREST, ILL.		188	79	38
ARMOUR, LESTER	ALTERATIONS		97	55	-
ARMOUR, LESTER	LAKE BLUFF, ILL.		218	91	45
ARMOUR, MRS. J. OGDEN, HOUSE	LAKE FOREST, ILL.		242	101 & 101-A	53
ARMOUR, MRS. J. OGDEN	LAKE FOREST, ILL. - SERVICE BLDGS		244	101-A	53
ARMSBY			-	3	-
ARMSTRONG			-	3	-
ATCHISON, TOPEKA & SANTA FE RY	DINING CAR		161	48	-
ATTIC CLUB	FIELD BUILDING	JOB # 163	236	95	-
AUSTRIAN, H.S.	CHICAGO				17
ARMOUR, A.W	APT. 1500 LAKE SHORE DRIVE	JOB # 189	147	94A	
ADLER, D.	MONTEREY CO, CALIFORNIA		94A		

A page in Adler's job book

which, with its symmetrical limestone façade, crowning mansard roof, and period detailing, replicated the grand mansions of late eighteenth-century Paris—his only townhouse design in this style. Annie Ryerson, like David Adler, was passionate about French architecture. But this time, she asked him to make alterations to her Santa Barbara house, El Cerrito, an Italian Renaissance villa, built in 1913 by her late father-in-law. She was the last client to talk to Adler about a new commission: she wrote in her diary on September 25, 1949, just two days before his death, "talked to David Adler today about doing over Santa Barbara." Adler had also planned another meeting with Paul and Ruth Winslow to discuss the finishing details of their house. But the meeting never took place. The Winslows were waiting in his office when news of his death reached them.

Frances Elkins orchestrated her brother's half-hour afternoon memorial service, which was held on December 1, 1949, in a gallery at the Art Institute of Chicago, where Adler had been a trustee since 1925. In addition to the contributions he had made during his lifetime, he left a substantial portion of his $500,000 estate to the museum. Frances's loving attention to detail was everywhere evident. Isabella Worn (1869–1950), San Francisco's society florist and horticulturist, and a friend of Elkins, arranged for every pale pink and rose-colored carnation in California to be flown to Chicago the morning of the service. Adler had been partial to flowers for decoration, using them as carefully placed accents in his rooms, and carnations were his favorite. A tree from the woods at his farmhouse in Libertyville, gilded, was placed on a platform at the end of the gallery. Fellow trustee, longtime friend, and client Alfred E. Hamill addressed Adler's family, friends, clients, and associates. As he spoke, a winter storm darkened the afternoon and a soft candlelight flickered from elegant silver candelabra, borrowed for the service. A quartet played before and after the service. Another of Adler's friends, Margaret Day Blake, wrote afterwards: "Looking back, one can see now what was not realized at the time because of being too absorbed in the death of a friend, that it was not only a farewell to David, but also symbolically an end of a social period. . . . The period when balance and proportion were requisites for gracious living is a memory of the past, except for the few who were part of that time."

After Adler's death, it fell to Frances Elkins to make the disposition of his 1860s farmhouse and its two hundred acres of property, which he had bought with Katherine in 1918. During the thirty years that Adler owned the property, he added constantly to it, changing it from a simple six-room clapboard Victorian to a stuccoed twenty-six room—though informal—country house. He added several bedrooms, a dining porch, a sitting room and a formal dining room, extending the house's original footprint to the east and the south. Adler's house was his laboratory where he experimented with a mixture of historic styles, including colonial, French Norman, and Greek revival—all found in several of his future commissions. It was Adler's ability to draw from the past, combining period details, which he flawlessly reproduced, with his own classical and predominantly symmetrical designs that made him the architect of choice.

The property was a testament to Adler. However, because Frances Elkins lived in California, she decided to give the farm to Libertyville as the David Adler Memorial Park. She asked William McCormick Blair, president of the Art Institute, longtime family friend Adler's hunting companion, and the trustee of his estate, to make the offer.

Blair continued, during his lifetime, to honor his close relationship with Adler in many ways. In the 1960s he organized the publication of the book *David Adler* by Richard Pratt. John Gregg Allerton, Adler's one-time draftsman and the adopted son of Chicago civic and social leader Robert Allerton, recalled that he and Blair contributed equal sums toward the book's publication, even though they thought that it wouldn't sell. Mr. Blair himself said that preparing the book had been difficult because Adler "kept few records."

In 1979, thirty years after Adler's death, Blair returned to Libertyville to intervene again in a special way. The three passing decades had not been kind to Adler's house and it needed extensive repairs. Intent on preserving his friend's memory and retaining the house's present use as a cultural center, Blair founded the David Adler Cultural Center in 1980. With funds that Blair raised, which included contributions from several of Adler's clients, the house was renovated. Blair also enlisted the help of Adler's great nephew and Frances Elkins's grandson, David Boyd, who is the keeper of the family archives and conservator of much of "Uncle David's" possessions. He enthusiastically donated his uncle's dining room furniture to the house. Hence, the dining room in the original part of the farmhouse, with its reinstalled Zuber wallcovering, was also restored in tribute to David Adler.

During his career, David Adler designed townhouses, apartments, clubhouses, and made additions and alterations to existing buildings. More than any other form, and most important, he designed country houses. These commissions ranged in architectural style from Early American to French provincial, and from bungalow to Georgian. The houses selected for inclusion here give a broad picture of the range and accomplishment of Adler's career. The sequence is chronological, by date of the initial architectural rendering.

Adler's Libertyville dining room

PART I

THE ADLER-DANGLER YEARS
1911–1917

Bringing European Grandeur to the American House

Top: View of house
from Lake Michigan

Above: Terrace façade

Opposite: View from
allée to house

Mr. and Mrs. Charles A. Stonehill

Glencoe, Illinois, 1911
Razed

David Adler's first client, Charles A. Stonehill, played a highly significant role in the aspiring young architect's life. Husband of Adler's maternal aunt, and a successful hat manufacturer, Stonehill had paid for his nephew's living expenses while he was studying in Paris. Adler reciprocated by designing for him a Louis XIII–style building, inspired by the Chateau de Balleroy in Normandy. Perched on a high bluff overlooking Lake Michigan, the Stonehill house was hailed by *Architectural Record* in 1912 as the finest country house of its scale in Chicago.

An elm-bordered drive led from a wrought-iron fence on Sheridan Road to the balustraded forecourt of the house. There a three-car garage and living quarters for the chauffeur and gardeners balanced an orangery with twin greenhouses. Symmetry guided Adler's design of the Stonehill house, providing an early hint of what would become a recognizable trademark.

For the handsome Stonehill façade Adler specified pink brick and limestone trim, which softened the house's imposing appearance. Its tall windows and steeply pitched roof typified French Normandy architecture. Adler planned the interior around a large entrance hall, which he detailed classically with a coffered ceiling, a checkered black-and-white marble floor, and fluted Corinthian pilasters. Furnished with Mediterranean pieces selected in Europe by Adler and the Stonehills, the hall was lit by Italian lanterns mounted on the pilasters, and massive wall tapestries conveyed a sense of spaciousness.

One end of the entrance hall led to the main stair hall, while the other opened into the music room through a pair of doors. Here, Louis XVI paneling and parquet-de-Versailles flooring set off the room's concert grand piano and Louis XV furnishings. A Gainsborough portrait hung over the fireplace.

At the back of the house, Adler placed a vaulted loggia that spanned three bays across the terrace and served as a repository for natural light,

Entrance hall

Music room

as well as an observatory from which to view the lake below. Reached by way of a keystoned arch-way from the entrance hall, the loggia joined the drawing room to the south and the dining room on the north. The dining room was paneled in English walnut and furnished in Mediterranean pieces, including a long, hand-carved walnut table and tall, upholstered high-back chairs. An Aubusson tapestry hung above the buffet.

In the drawing room, Adler blended classi-cal detailing with Mediterranean decor by repeating the coffered ceiling of the entrance hall and lining the room with Tuscan pilasters. The ceiling was unique; imported from Europe by Adler, its octagonal-shaped coffers were decorated with colorful Italian paintings of angelic figures. A large screened porch con-nected to the drawing room and opened onto the terrace, overlooking the formal garden and the lake.

Upstairs, at the end of the curved white marble staircase, a windowed hallway provided a view over the bluff to Lake Michigan. Paralleling the loggia on the first floor, the hall-way led to the master suite and the family and guest bedrooms, each accompanied by a capa-cious bathroom.

Adler's lifelong interest in the grounds of his houses was already evident in here. Illinois landscape architect Jens Jensen (1860–1951)

Dining room

Drawing room

designed three distinctive gardens. The north-west corner of the property, edging Sheridan Road, sprouted a vegetable garden, and squabs were raised in the nearby poultry coop. Across the forecourt, the orangery opened south onto the greenhouses and cutting garden and east to the formal French garden, which, with its geometrically-patterned flower beds and gravel walkways, edged the house and its elevated lakeside terrace.

A wide flight of stone steps connected the garden to the balustraded terrace and its well-manicured lawn. A gravel walkway divided the shrub-lined lawn into four identical quarters, expanding the symmetrical plan of the house and gardens, and the terrace afforded spectacular views of Lake Michigan. Like many of Adler's future houses, the Stonehill commission represented a dramatic union of site and architectural élan.

The Stonehill family lived at Pierremont, as they named the estate, until the late 1920s. Following the Crash, however, the house was taken over by the bank. Eventually Syma Busiel, co-founder of Lady Esther Cosmetics, purchased the house and lived there until the early 1960s, when she sold it to North Shore Congregation Israel as the site for their new synagogue. It was the fourth of seven Adler buildings to be demolished.

Entrance façade

Chateau de Montgiron

Mr. and Mrs. Ralph H. Poole

Lake Bluff, Illinois, 1912
Standing

When Adler and Dangler left the office of Howard Shaw, the portrait painter Abram Poole, an old classmate of Adler's from Princeton, helped the partnership win its first major commission. Abram's older brother Ralph, a commodities trader, and his wife Marie, were the clients. Their house, a chateau in the style of Louis XV, was to be set on forty secluded acres off Green Bay Road in Lake Bluff. The charge was to create a house that had the "charm and spontaneity of the wonderful French houses of the period" while also meeting "American conditions perfectly." Ralph Poole favored French architecture; both the Pooles agreed about who would furnish the interior: Adler and Abram Poole, in conjunction with William J. Quigley and Company, Chicago's preeminent upholsterer and maker of fine furniture.

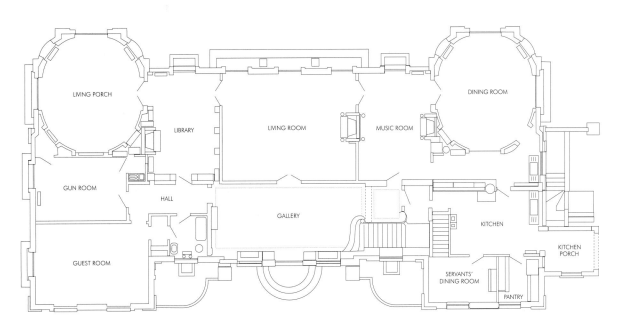

For inspiration, Adler drew heavily from the works of François Mansart (1598–1666), the forefather of classical French architecture. The strongest specific influence on the Poole house was the Chateau de Montgiron of Veilleins in the Loire Valley. Like its inspiration, the Poole house was symmetrical, with a pair of wings projecting subtly into the driveway's forecourt to balance the center section of the house. The Chateau de Montgiron was built in red brick; Adler chose a softer plaster wash to complement the exterior elevation's most prominent feature: full-length windows spanning the length of the ground floor. Rococo details in alternating patterns of cast cement faces and fanciful trim crowned the segmental curves atop these windows and thematically united the entire façade. Cast cement quoins, designed to resemble pilasters, reached toward the roof's edge. There, the series of dormer windows and four fruit-filled urns in cast cement added a sense of height to the center section of the house and drew attention to the main façade. The Poole house profile rose to an attractive slate mansard roof with low, horizontal lines.

The Hôtel Biron (once the home and studio of Auguste Rodin, now the Musée Rodin) was an important influence on Adler's plan for the interior of the Poole house. Adler loosely followed the configuration of the hôtel's entrance hallway, with its checkered floor and monumental stone staircase. Natural light flooding through a pair of full-length mullioned windows, a thirteen-foot ceiling, and a mirrored panel on the south wall all gave the hall an expansive quality. Surrounding the doorway that led into the living room was a plaster relief depicting the "Four Arts," echoing the rococo ornamentation of the exterior.

Adler placed the five principal rooms enfilade along the rear of the house. Opposite the living porch and the library on the south side were the dining room and the music room. At the center of the grouping, serving as its nucleus, was the living room. Here, again, natural light reflected from a charcoal-hued terrazzo floor and illuminated the ornamentation of the plastered wall panels. The fireplace mantel

Staircase in Hôtel Biron, Paris

Opposite: Entrance hall

was of aubergine-colored marble, and above it was set a mirrored panel of French inspiration.

The living room flowed naturally into the intimately scaled interiors of the music room and the dining room. In the music room, rococo ornamentation, appropriately based on the theme of musical instruments, decorated the partially paneled walls. An *Architectural Forum* article of April 1922 that discussed the collaborative designs of the Adler-Dangler partnership described the original decoration of the music room as "painted yellow with green lines, the rest of the walls being covered with old yellow damask." A pair of identical mirrored panels and a cove ceiling added spaciousness. On the projecting chimney breast of the fireplace wall, the over-mantel mirror exchanged reflections with

a counterpart on the opposite wall. Here Adler at once maintained symmetry in the music room and, at the same time, concealed the chimney breast of the adjacent living room, which projected on this wall, by creating the illusion that the room contained two fireplaces.

The music room connected with the oval-shaped, light-filled dining room, certainly the most beautiful room in the house. During the day, a panoramic view of the estate appeared through the succession of French windows that encircled the room's paneled walls. As the view faded into the evening light, the glass windowpanes reflected the room's terrazzo floor.

Opposite the music and dining rooms lay the library and living porch. More sober detailing distinguished the library from the other principal rooms. For example, with the exception of the curvilinear outline in the over-mantel panels of the fireplace, the library's walls, paneled in natural gum, were detailed in a straight-edged pattern. Adding a typically French touch, Adler specified grilled doors for the bookcases. The cove ceiling, at twelve feet, was the lowest in the house, giving the room intimacy and warmth.

Adjoining the library was the living porch, oval like the dining room opposite it. Though the living porch was intended as a family space, its detailing was treated as carefully as that in the more formal dining room. Straight-edged panels outlined the white plaster walls, and instead of terrazzo, the floor was paved in red tile. Rodin's Hôtel Biron terminated in oval rooms overlooking a lush garden. With this in mind, Adler's plan called for encircling French windows that rendered the porch an ideal garden room where family and friends could gather before dinner to relax and enjoy the soothing sounds of the fountain that spilled into a small goldfish pool. Beyond lay the garden and fields. Turning away from the scenic beauty through the French windows, the viewer's gaze falls upon the enfilade, the entire length of the house: library, living room, music room, and dining room, all coming together in an expansive and carefully arranged progression Adler clearly understood French design.

The plan for the second floor of the house utilized the full footprint of the first floor (excluding the ellipses of the dining room and the living porch) and included a master bedroom, four family bedrooms, and three full

bathrooms. A service wing off a rear hall contained a sewing room and three maid's rooms. Marie Poole held Adler in high regard as both friend and accomplished architect. She had but one complaint: though he was "good with the grand rooms," she told her eldest child, Barbara White, he was eminently impractical in the provision of adequate closet space. Even after she asked Adler to provide additional closets, his response was to design a pair of wardrobes for her dressing room that barely accommodated a fraction of her clothes. As she loved to quip, because a man had planned her bedroom closets, she had to hang many of her dresses in a hall cupboard at the opposite end of the house.

As with the Stonehill house, Adler gave nearly the same degree of attention to the Pooles' grounds as he did to the house. Along the southern elevation, beneath the living porch, lay the garden. Frederick Law Olmsted's renowned Boston landscape firm was commissioned to plan the garden, though, according to Roger Baldwin, a nephew of the Pooles, the Olmsted design never materialized. Presumably Adler had his hand in the landscape design: a grass terrace introduced the garden in perfect alignment with the south elevation of the house. A pair of steps on alternate ends of the terrace gave way to the garden, where the lawn was dotted with fruit trees and bordered by flower-lined beds of colorful lilacs and peonies. The inside edge of these beds formed yet another border for the garden's center court, which gradually sloped to a lower level.

A field of alfalfa and clover created a natural backdrop for the handsome rear elevation, with its trellised center block balanced by the rounded bays of the dining room and living porch. According to Barbara White and her brother, Richard Poole, the field contributed to the utilitarian needs of the estate. Several times a year, the field was mowed and the harvest used to feed the half-dozen cows that were kept in the somewhat distant barn. (The barn also housed the children's horse, a pig, and Ralph Poole's collection of Japanese Silkie chickens.) The barn and neighboring gardener's cottage were built before the main house, and the Pooles lived there during the construction.

Though the gardener's cottage and the barn were both lost in a fire, the main house remained in the family until 1976, when Carl and Sandy Zapffe purchased the estate from Nancy Poole Rich and her husband. Today, the original forty acres has diminished to eight, without loss of privacy for the estate.

The Poole house marked the beginnings of a flourishing partnership for David Adler and Henry Dangler. Adler and Dangler's professional association produced sixteen houses of English, French, and Italian derivation. *Architectural Forum* noted that the partnership's designs represented a distinct improvement in American domestic architecture and introduced in this country "a more scholarly study of precedent."

Entrance façade,
Berney house

Mr. and Mrs. Morris E. Berney

Fort Worth, Texas, 1915
Standing

Entrance façade,
Anderson house

Six of the houses produced by the Adler-Dangler partnership were inspired by Mediterranean architecture, perhaps because the majority of the commissions came from temperate locales. Adler's design of a neighboring pair of Italian Renaissance villas (1915–16) in Fort Worth, Texas, marked the beginning of his interest in this style. Built by Morris and Flora Berney for themselves and Mrs. Berney's mother, Elizabeth Anderson, these two houses were the only ones that Adler executed simultaneously for a family compound—a nearly one-hundred-acre site that was part of the River Crest Country Club, of which Morris Berney was a charter member.

The connection between Adler and the Berneys is as interesting as the commission that it yielded. It started with cotton, in which Mr. Berney traded, requiring that he and his wife

spend a fair amount of time in Chicago. Flora Berney was a world traveler and an "arbiter of taste," which ensured that she would meet several of the city's prominent families—including the Armours and the Marshall Fields, who were her entrée to Adler.

The Berney commission presented a distinct challenge for Adler. Because the two houses were to be built in close proximity, he had to be especially sensitive to their exteriors, allowing them to relate to each other without diminishing their individuality. As usual, symmetry was the guiding principle of his design, and he applied it, along with such typically Mediterranean features as a textured façade and red tile roof, as the unifying links between the two houses. Size—the Berney house was larger—and the principal detailing distinguished one house from the other. For example, their entrance fronts were completely differ-

ent. For the Berneys' house, Adler edged the fifty-foot-long stuccoed center block with an arcaded loggia, while he set off the entry door of Mrs. Anderson's against a pilastered apron of limestone that contrasted effectively with the cement-washed brick façade.

The Berney property remained in the family until 1937, when Mrs. Anderson's heirs sold her house to William and Jewel Bomar. After Flora Berney died, her husband, who remarried, continued to live in their house until his death in 1948. His widow sold the villa shortly thereafter.

William and Jewel Bomar were also clients of Adler's. They had hired him in 1920 to design a house within the confines of the River Crest Country Club. However, they abandoned their plans, eventually buying the Anderson house instead. Today, both houses remain, lovingly cared for by their owners.

Garden façade

Entrance façade of Villa Turicum (Charles A. Platt, architect), Lake Forest, Illinois

Mr. and Mrs. Charles B. Pike

Lake Forest, Illinois, 1916
Standing

The Fort Worth commissions set the tone for six similar houses that Adler would design during his career, even in climates unlike that of Texas. Among them was the impressive Lake Forest villa of Charles and Frances Pike, built in 1916. No doubt the villa's proximity to Lake Michigan contributed to the successful use of the Italian style. Certainly on Adler's mind as he designed the Pike house was Villa Turicum, one of Lake Forest's most prominent houses. Owned by Harold and Edith Rockefeller McCormick, Villa Turicum (1908) was designed by Charles A. Platt, one of the great domestic architects of the twentieth century, who had a strong feeling for the Italian Renaissance garden. Adler had a high regard for Platt's designs: a 1913 monograph on Platt was in his architectural library.

Villa Turicum overlooked Lake Michigan,

Entrance façade

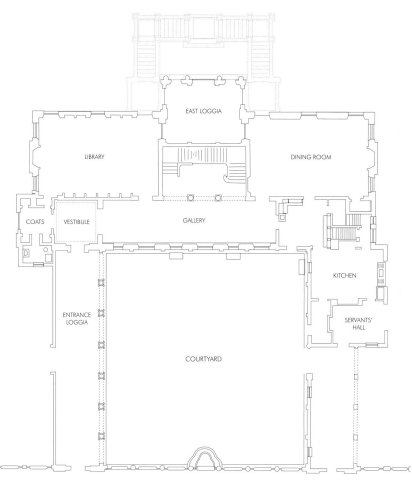

with its entrance elevation facing west. Adler reversed Platt's plan, turning the Pike villa's red-tiled, flat hip roof toward the lake. The rear loggia edged a paved courtyard surrounded by tall brick walls that separated the back of the house from the road. The courtyard was one of Adler's most successful outdoor spaces. Paving it with a variety of stones from the beachfront below, he created an interplay of color, texture, and shape. At the center of the courtyard a large star in shades of black and dark tan was encircled by a guilloche and connected to four evenly spaced rectangular stone paths that separated four corner planting beds—which Adler fit, with the precision of a jigsaw puzzle, into the courtyard.

Adler's plan also effectively integrated the courtyard with the interior space. Three sets of French doors opened directly from the courtyard into the vaulted gallery. Pilaster-supported

Courtyard

Opposite, top: Living room

Opposite, bottom: Dining room

archways crowned these doorways, as well as the series of four windows that separated them, adding depth to the plaster-washed façade of pink-buff brick.

The interior plan of the Pike house was simple and concise. Inside the front door, opening north into the cloakroom and south to the gallery, was a compact vestibule, with a single vault in its ceiling. The fifty-foot-long gallery, with its balanced pair of Tuscan columns and a fifteen-foot ceiling, was expansive. The limestone columns introduced the double-height stair hall, which was centered on the principal axis of the house. The cut limestone of the staircase and surrounding walls anchored the wrought-iron railing that extended to the second-floor gallery, where a black-and-white cement checkered floor and a cove ceiling connected the bedroom wings.

The first floor contained three main rooms —the "library" (the name Adler gave the living room), the dining room, and the east loggia— all oriented toward the east, facing Lake Michigan. The first room off the gallery, the living room, was rectangular, with a fifteen-foot vaulted ceiling and a black stone mantel above the fireplace that was the focal point of the room. Over five feet in height, the mantel consisted of a broad shelf supported by a pair of pilasters adorned with delicate carved tracery, while on the face of the mantel shelf a small Grecian bust was embossed on its two lower corners. The furniture of the library was arranged to give views of the lake and the fireplace.

Identical in size to the living room, the dining room served to balance the spatial relationships on the first floor. Though paved with the same black terrazzo that Adler used in the gallery and living room, Adler created a greater sense of intimacy with a lower, beamed ceiling and by covering most of the terrazzo floor with an Oriental rug.

Projecting from the center of the house toward the formal gardens, the east loggia was situated directly behind the main stair hall and connected to the living room and the dining room through generous French doors. A tall vaulted ceiling and white marble flooring amplified the room's bright and airy feeling. A second pair of French doors opened onto the balustraded landings of a pair of staircases lead-

ing down to the garden. Adler planned the sunken garden in collaboration with Illinois landscape architect Ralph Rodney Root (1884–1964). The grandest of Adler's lakefront gardens, it would be exceeded in magnificence only by the allée at Castle Hill, created by Boston landscape architect Arthur Shurcliff (1870–1957).

Walled and well manicured, the sunken lawn was outlined on each side by interlocking clusters of yews that were tailored and trimmed to form a square-edged geometric pattern along most of the length of the lawn. The shrubbery ended at another pair of balustraded steps that led to the upper garden. Beyond the steps, the sunken lawn bordered the bluff rising above Lake Michigan. A side path led from the bluff to the beachfront below where a flower garden dotted the water's edge.

The house included a garden room that opened onto the sunken level of the garden, and a connecting ship room whose vaulted interior, with its explicit nautical theme, was obviously intended for fun and pleasure. A model of a large sailing ship hung from the center of the ceiling, and models of sailboats as well as related photographs and memorabilia were mounted on the walls. And for bitter Chicago winter days, a fireplace set into the north wall aligned with the living room fireplace above.

The Pike house was the last of the Adler–Dangler partnership.

*Hamill garden pavilion,
detail*

PART II

ADLER EXPANDS
1917–1929

Building Classical Character and Spacious Domains

Entrance façade

Mr. and Mrs. Walter F. Dillingham

Honolulu, Hawaii, 1920
Standing

La Pietra, Florence, Italy

One of the earliest commissions that Adler received during his association with Robert Work came from Walter and Louise Dillingham. Though Louise was from Chicago, after she married, she and her husband settled in Honolulu, where the Dillingham family was prominent. The Dillinghams were married in 1910 at La Pietra, an Italian Renaissance villa owned by Louise's Aunt Hortense and Uncle Arthur Acton. It was the Acton villa, as well as the de Medici villa and the Villa Gambreia, also in Florence, that inspired Louise to build a La Pietra in Hawaii.

The Dillingham commission must have been challenging for Adler. It was far from his Chicago base, and he did not visit the site until after the house was built; he had to rely on plot plans sent to him by Walter Dillingham. During

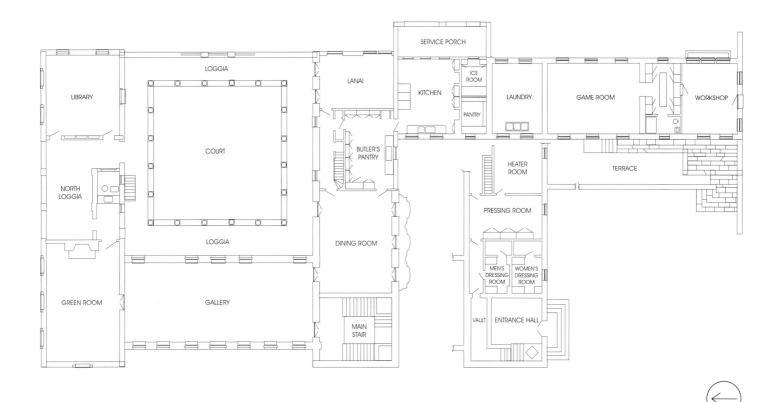

the design and construction of La Pietra, Adler and his clients communicated by means of letters and telegrams, most addressing the difficulties in building the house. Preparing the ten-acre site for construction was a feat in itself. Diamond Head was uncharted territory in the 1920s. Dillingham's crew had to lay roads and install public utilities and storm drains. A 1920 memorandum to Adler that accompanied a contour map of the site described the property in detail, including its entrance: "Entrance to the property is at the southwest corner, where a 100 ft. right of way connects the property with the boulevard through the public park (Kapiolani). Above the property rises the prominent landmark Diamond Head."

The roads within the boundaries of the Dillingham property ran in several directions. Initially the main drive proceeded due north,

but before reaching the property's lower field it became an inverted S-curve that gradually climbed the hill toward Diamond Head. At the final leg of the drive the road diverged, with one fork continuing east to the garage court below Diamond Head and the other running north through a rolling lawn of olive trees to the entrance forecourt.

The Italian Renaissance provided the governing influence for La Pietra. A reddish ceramic tile covered its flat hip roof, while a pink wash softened the plastered façade of hand-hewn volcanic stone, Florentine in its rusticated arched surround at the front door. As at the Acton villa in Florence, round heads capped the three windows that overlooked the forecourt from the first-floor dining room. Bluish-green shutters flanked these windows, and they were also fronted by a wrought-iron balcony. The

Green Room

contrasting colors of pink, green, and black added visual texture to the façade.

The views from La Pietra were spectacular in every direction: Diamond Head, the Koolau Range, and the Pacific Ocean. Adler's plan took full advantage of the property's varied grades. At ground level, the walnut double front door opened from the forecourt into the fourteen-square-foot entrance hall, given enhanced verticality by a triple-height vaulted stairwell. The herringbone-patterned brick floor and stone staircase of the hall was Mediterranean in character. On the first floor, the gallery, dining room, "Green Room," and library surrounded three sides of a large outdoor courtyard measuring thirty-eight feet square. The gallery formed one side of the courtyard, opening on opposite sides into the Green Room and the dining room. The gallery's floor was paved in a herringbone terra-cotta tile. French doors opened from both sides of the gallery onto the courtyard loggia and the west terrace, which faced Waikiki. A loggia on the north side of the house also connected with the Green Room

and the library. The Green Room, named for its pea-colored walls, was the most formal room in the house. Here, crystal chandeliers cast sparkling light on Chinese rugs in shades of gold, yellow, and blue and on the antique furniture.

Because Walter Dillingham, as chairman of the Hawaii Emergency Labor Commission (which monitored labor conditions in Hawaii) spent a fair amount of time in Washington, D.C., there was an abundance of written correspondence between husband and wife. While building La Pietra, Louise kept Walter well informed of the details and the progress. According to their son Ben, Walter did not know Adler very well, but he wanted Louise to be happy, and so he went along with her plans, offering his advice and opinions on every aspect of the house. Structural details were important to Dillingham, who was concerned about earthquakes and therefore requested especially thick walls. Consequently, the foundation walls were built fifteen feet thick and, needless to say, La Pietra has fared well amidst nature's challenges.

Dining room

As usual, Adler was sensitive to the house's context. The central courtyard was an extension of the first floor and provided an easy flow between the interior and exterior spaces. The gallery, dining room, and library all opened onto the arcaded loggia, which surrounded the courtyard on all four sides with its sandstone columns. Family and friends could lounge beneath the vaulted ceilings, protected from the ever-present Hawaiian sun, or step down to the courtyard and its marble garden pool and fountain. Originally, Japanese moss covered the courtyard surface, but the moss was too difficult to maintain and the court was eventually repaved with coral stone. Petunia-filled planters and pots splashed the courtyard with color.

Outdoor living at La Pietra was not limited to the courtyard. On the luxuriant grounds were a tennis court and a swimming pool, both overlooked by Diamond Head. A set of wrought-iron gates opened east from the courtyard loggia to a gated flight of steps that climbed the walled embankment to the swimming pool. The pool was rectangular and faced

in white tile. Surrounding the pool was a terrace of coral stone, framed by an expansive area of lawn. The landscaping around the pool was distinctly tropical: pomegranate trees intertwined, trellis-like, with the surrounding stone walls, whose plastered facing had been dotted with a uniform series of oval-shaped portholes to accommodate the trees. The tennis court area was set directly into the side of the landmark crater.

A lawn hedged by hibiscus and a set of stone steps separated the tennis court, which was built on a lower grade, from the pool. A stone wall surrounded the court, and stone benches were placed intermittently around the court. On the Diamond Head side, two rows of gallery seating overlooked the court, which in turn overlooked the allée of grass that extended from the villa's north loggia. A balustraded stone staircase set into the property's walled embankment led from the tennis court to a garden path, which opened onto the allée. The staircase was imposing with its double flight of steps resembling a spread eagle projecting from the

Gallery

wall and sweeping down in opposite directions to the path. Stone statues depicting the four seasons lined the railing, while geometric designs in umber offset the pink-hued walls.

Another span of walls fronted the garden path and opened in line with the staircase, forming the entrance to the walled allée. At first, a screen of hibiscus hedges was used to enclose the allée, but because they proved too difficult to maintain, the hedges were replaced. Adler's ingenious plan created the perfect alternative to the lost greenery: the stone walls resembled a box shrub, which, when covered with ficus vines, looked like a Florentine hedge. The vines grew heartily, though it took a decade before the full effect was realized. Indeed, the fully covered stone walls were lush and harmonious with the landscape and contributed greater strength and definition to the allée. Unlike the hibiscus, the stone hedges were visually impenetrable and their tall and stately posture enhanced the treasured sense of privacy in this garden setting. The walls also framed the villa's north elevation, whose pink-hued plaster façade, red-tiled roof, and arcaded loggia contrasted with the green shutters on the second-floor windows and a variety of umber-shaded geometric ornamentation around the windows and the loggia archways.

Adler's plan for La Pietra included a complex of two farm buildings on a lower field. Stone steps led west from an arbor gate down to these buildings, which consisted of a one-story cottage and an adjacent L-shaped barn. The cottage accommodated the resident gardener and the barn stalls housed the Jersey cows that provided heavy cream for the family. Both buildings were designed in the Mediterranean style with red-tiled roofs and rough plastered façades in sky blue.

Walter Dillingham's polo ponies were housed adjacent to his lower field in Kapiolani Park at the Hawaii Polo and Racing Club, of which Dillingham was a charter member. In writing to a friend about the recent completion of La Pietra, he mentioned how easy it was for him and his four children to "keep up and take up horseback riding." The house quickly became the epicenter of social life on the Hawaiian Islands and was characterized as "open and informal." The Dillinghams' hospitality was renowned and visitors were numerous, including couples on their honeymoon in Honolulu, who received a telephone call from Louise inviting them for cocktails. Every week saw a party to welcome the interesting and important visitors who came by ship to Honolulu. These parties were often hosted in the courtyard, from which the guests could watch the moon rise over Diamond Head.

For more than four decades, La Pietra was the home and base of the Dillingham family. Walter Dillingham died in 1963, deeding the villa and its remaining five acres (the other five were developed into townhouses) to Honolulu's Punahou School, his alma mater; Louise Dillingham had the right to live at the villa for her lifetime, but she "lost her zest for life" and died three months later. Ben Dillingham recalled that his mother had once envisioned La Pietra as a historic monument that could have been used as the governor's mansion. The Dillinghams hoped that Punahou would make La Pietra a campus. At first, several members of the faculty and their families lived at the villa, but because Diamond Head was too far from the school's Honolulu location, the school decided to sell the property. Hawaii School for Girls bought La Pietra in 1968 and within a year, after adapting the house for its new use, moved from its initial Honolulu site, the Central Union Church. The school has flourished, graduating eight hundred students as of the year 2000. Activity abounds in the villa and in the buildings that have been added through the years. Classrooms now stand on what was once the swimming pool area, and nearby are a science building and a gymnasium that was built into the embankment, resulting in a roofline that runs parallel with the upper slopes of Diamond Head.

La Pietra remains a landmark on the island of Oahu. Its transformation into a school was fortuitous, fulfilling, in a sense, Louise Dillingham's wish for its destiny.

Entrance façade

Mr. and Mrs. Alfred E. Hamill

Lake Forest, Illinois, 1917
Standing

Although commissions for country houses dominated Adler's career, he was often called upon to renovate or design additions to houses that he had not built. One of these commissions was an Italian-style house designed by Henry Dangler in 1914 in Lake Forest for investment banker Alfred Hamill and his wife Clarice. Dangler and Hamill were first cousins and close friends; they had attended Yale together. Dangler had introduced Adler to Hamill, and over the course of time, Adler and Hamill became good friends as well. Hamill, a trustee of the Art Institute of Chicago, was responsible for Adler's involvement with the museum.

Hamill's sons, Ernest and Corwith, remember their father's house as a "continuous" project, reflecting Hamill's changing tastes from around 1917 through the 1920s. When Adler became involved, the Hamill house took on a grander look. The changes started at the foot of the driveway: a pair of pedestaled bronze centaurs introduced a new forecourt, paved in brick with limestone trim, replacing the original circular turnaround. The greatest alteration to the entrance block, however, was made at the roofline, where a false parapet heightened the house and screened its red tiled-roof.

Adler directed changes inside the house as well. First, a single-bay garage, designed for an electric automobile, was transformed into a breakfast room. A few years later, the living porch, originally reached through the living room, was converted into a music room, and a spacious library was added. Connected to the living room and the music room, the library also balanced the east wing, which held the kitchen. A set of limestone steps led from the living room down to the library. Hamill was a

Library

bibliophile and the new room catered to this special interest. He asked illustrator Thomas M. Cleland (1880–1964) to design a new bookplate that depicted the centaurs of his new forecourt. Hamill loved the plate, and its signature, so to speak, in over eight thousand volumes of his prompted him to rename his estate, formerly Villino Saint Nicola, to Centaurs.

The library was warm and inviting, despite its imposing contents. Tall bookcases in walnut lined the walls and the hemispherical niche between a pair of doors at the room's north end. One door opened to the music room, while the other concealed a spiral staircase that led to Hamill's second-floor bedroom. Adler's typically precise classical detailing started at the fireplace, where a surround of black marble and limestone was crowned by an open pedimented mantel. The walls above the bookcases were

lined with evenly spaced keystone arches, which sprang from the tops of the bookcases and connected to the cornice. Near each corner of the library the arches became recessed niches, framing the principal doorways.

According to Ernest Hamill, the archway atop the doorway at the library's south end had produced a problematic effect: its curvature created an optical illusion, causing the ceiling to appear to bend down in each corner. To correct this misperception, Adler added round niches just below the cornice on either side of the doorway. In each he placed a limestone bust— one of Homer and one of Shakespeare—which raised the viewer's eye and counteracted the illusion. To balance these, Adler also added the niches at the north end of the room.

Off the library another room was added to house the stacks, providing additional space for

Garden pavilion

Hamill's book collection. The stacks and the library formed an ell that created, outdoors, an intimate walled courtyard for Clarice Hamill's "yellow garden." Here yews manicured in a geometric pattern outlined a brick-paved terrace dotted with lemon-hued marigolds in white pots.

Hamill continued to improve his estate through the late 1920s, adding a garage and tower building and a garden pavilion. The pavilion was built at the end of the principal garden, on axis with the house. Palladian in design, the limestone open summerhouse, with its terrace of terrazzo and stone, offered a tranquil spot to rest and simply enjoy the setting. Above was a railed deck reached by narrow circular steps that spiraled around a pair of cylindrical posts on each side of the pavilion. Identical bronze sculptures of a draped lady by John Storrs, a student of Rodin, stood atop each post. Ernest Hamill said that these intricate double staircases of poured reinforced concrete were "very expensive"; the Hamill's Swedish contractor lamented that "they cost more money than his house."

The garage and servants' quarters sat away from the house, edging Mayflower Road. Italianate in design, like the original house, the whitewashed brick building consisted of a long two-story structure with a red-tiled roof and a tower at its southern end. (The elevation facing Mayflower Road was especially reminiscent of Italy, with its arcade of seven evenly spaced concrete arches.) The three arches closest to the tower stood sentry to three garages, which, together, served as balance to the gardener's apartment at the opposite end of the building. Above the garage were accommodations for the Hamills' chauffeur: an apartment with two bedrooms, a bathroom, and a kitchen (the kitchen occupied the second floor of the tower).

Almost seventy-five feet tall, the tower was unique. Its six floors were connected by a staircase that originated in the garage workshop on the ground floor. Above the chauffeur's kitchen were a playroom for Ernest and Corwith, a private study for Mr. Hamill, a guest suite, and an "open room" on the tower's roof. The rooms in the tower were not large—the block measured only twenty-four feet square, including the stairwell that hugged the tower's perimeter as it ascended. Hamill's study, according to Ernest, was austere; its walls and vaulted ceiling were completely covered with a monochromatic mural by the Russian expatriate artist Nikolai Remisoff (1887–1975), whose use of murky dark-brown hues to depict Byzantine figures was only occasionally relieved by touches of gold and white and a trompe-l'oeil curtain below. What Ernest Hamill remembered most clearly, however, were the unimpeded views from the open top room of the tower: Lake Michigan, downtown Chicago on a clear day, and the Bahai Temple in Wilmette.

In 1945 Adler completed one final project for Alfred Hamill: an addition to Elsewhere, Hamill's one-room retreat built during the late 1920s twenty miles northwest of Lake Forest. Adler added a French Provincial master bedroom suite and electricity and running water.

Hamill died in 1953. Within a year, Clarice Hamill sold Centaurs. Today the house is still privately owned, but the garden pavilion and tower are a separate property, the tower building converted into a single-family residence.

Tower building

Alfred Hamill's study

Mr. and Mrs. Jesse L. Strauss

Glencoe, Illinois, 1921
Interiors with Frances Elkins
Standing

Above: Terrace façade

*Opposite: Strauss house,
entrance façade*

The Stonehill house in Glencoe won Adler two more clients there. Banker Harold Foreman asked Adler to renovate his Howard Shaw house, which had been badly damaged by fire in 1920. The house was part of a compound of four Shaw houses built during the teens by Edgar Born, Foreman's father-in-law. Adler enlarged the Foreman house, changing it from English country to French Normandy manor and giving it a turreted front that related well to the seventeenth-century French farmhouse across the road that Adler designed, in 1921, for Foreman's first cousin, hat manufacturer Jesse Strauss.

Adler's partiality towards this use of the turreted front was apparent as early as 1918, when he began the first of many alterations to his own nineteenth-century farmhouse in Libertyville. Included in his plans for that year was the addition

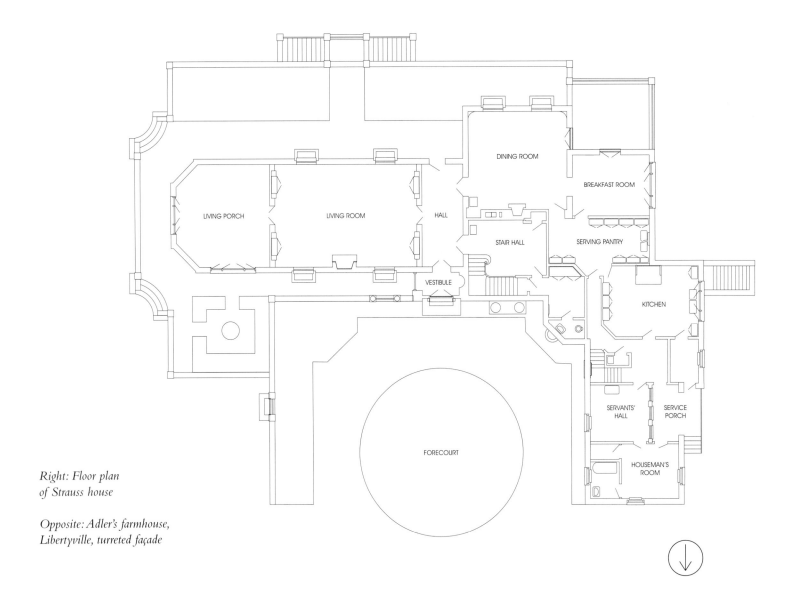

DINING ROOM

BREAKFAST ROOM

LIVING PORCH

LIVING ROOM

HALL

SERVING PANTRY

STAIR HALL

KITCHEN

VESTIBULE

SERVANTS'
HALL

SERVICE
PORCH

FORECOURT

HOUSEMAN'S
ROOM

*Right: Floor plan
of Strauss house*

*Opposite: Adler's farmhouse,
Libertyville, turreted façade*

of a servants' cottage with an anchoring polygonal tower. With Norman architecture fresh on
his mind, it is not surprising that Adler adapted
the style for the Foreman and Strauss commissions.

Access to the Strauss property was informal: a gated white-picket fence that opened
onto an entrance court led to a coach house,
whose stucco façade, arched garage doors, and
steeply pitched roof hinted at the architecture
of the main house. The coach house contained
a chauffeur's room and tool house on the first
floor, and a gardener's apartment upstairs.

Opposite the front of the coach house but
closer to the road was a potting house with a
connecting greenhouse that opened onto the
estate's cutting garden, where fruit trees outlined the rectangular garden. An orchard of crab
apple and cherry trees bordered by lilac dotted

the lawn between the garden and the service
wing of the house. The gardens were especially
important to Jesse Strauss, an accomplished horticulturist who raised tulips, camellias, begonias,
and prize-winning dahlias in the greenhouse. In
fact, according to his former daughter-in-law
Barbara, it was he who taught his gardeners
how to cultivate them.

East of the cutting garden, a long elm-tree-
lined entrance driveway, on axis with the house,
connected the entrance court with the formal
walled forecourt and created a sense of privacy.
Fruit trees filled the brick-lined planting beds
that edged this pastoral French farmhouse.
Brickwork that originated at the entrance court
and continued along the drive to the forecourt
unified the ensemble.

The focal point of the house's asymmetrical
design was its turreted front. Rising from the

corner of the L-shaped building, a tall polygonal tower formed part of the house's projecting entrance pavilion, which was defined by a sweeping gable and the steep pitched roofline typical of Norman architecture. Adler lowered the roofline on the ell, which housed the service quarters, giving greater prominence to the principal wing of the house, with its pair of Norman oeil-de-boeuf dormers. The walls were sand-colored stucco that blended well with the surroundings and contrasted effectively with the marine blue-and-white shutters and accompanying trim.

On the east side of the house Adler set a formal English garden connected to the entrance forecourt through a gated opening in the wall. The geometrically patterned rose garden was fronted by virgin woods that stretched to the main road. A walk dotted with wildflowers led from the garden through the woods, providing rustic routes to the entrance drive, coach house, and main road.

In Beaux-Arts tradition, the relationship of house and garden was an important component of Adler's plan. The rectangular garden was centered on the east terrace. A balanced pair of curved steps led from the garden to the flagstone terrace, which served as a forecourt for the bay-windowed living porch and continued to the rear of the house. Here its walled perimeter opened onto a double flight of steps that led down to a lower lawn and neighboring wooded ravine. Adler clearly capitalized on the property's varied grades; using the terrace's tall retaining walls for a foundation, he sited the house to appear as if it stood on a pedestal that grew out of the land.

The interior of the Strauss house—the first Chicago collaboration of Adler and Frances Elkins—had the informality, warmth, and comfort of a French farmhouse. Adler's plan for the interior was orderly: A center hall opened on axis to the rear terrace, led to the living room, main stair hall, and dining room. The living room looked onto the forecourt and the terrace, while the dining room, which was across the hall from the living room, projected onto the terrace. Rust-colored provincial tile paved the way from the center hall into the stair hall.

The beamed living room, with four corner breakfronts holding Delft china, and furniture

Opposite: Living room, sofa added by daughter-in-law

Left: Dining room

upholstered with French country print fabrics, was a study in blue and white. Stucco walls, wide plank floors, and a Delft-tiled baseboard set off the provincial antiques, among them an eighteenth-century card table and butler's table and a Louis XV sideboard that had been selected by the Strausses in France.

In the adjacent living porch, Adler lined the walls with tall French doors that opened onto the terrace, framed a generous view of the rose garden, and allowed natural light to pour in. For Adler, living porches provided the integral link between interior and exterior spaces.

The dining room wall panels, painted in alternate shades of dark and light taupe, framed the eighteenth-century hand-painted wallpaper that depicted an idyllic nature scene in earth tones. A Moroccan area rug in similar tones complemented the room's French provincial pieces—a fruitwood dining table and accompanying raffia-seated chairs. A pair of settees balanced each other, half-rounded backs nestled into the room's two curved corners. Reflected light danced off a pair of mirrored wall panels and a collection of copper accessories, clustered on the marble-topped sideboard and demilune tables.

Upstairs, in addition to the master suite and the child's bedroom, were guest rooms and a sleeping porch that overlooked the rear lawn. Almost forty years after the house was built, it became home for the next generation of Strausses.

62 CRANE

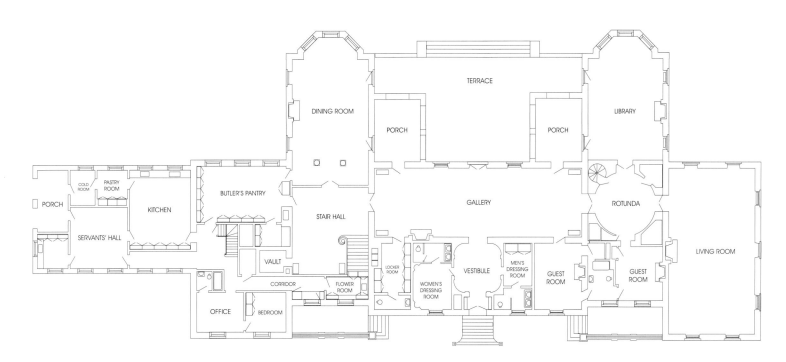

Mr. and Mrs. Richard T. Crane, Jr.

Ipswich, Massachusetts, 1924
Standing

By the early 1920s, Adler had established a following in Chicago and on Lake Michigan's North Shore, but he was always ready to tackle another region. In 1923 Adler designed an Italian Renaissance villa for Lloyd and Agnes Smith in Milwaukee; the location of his next out-of-town commission was Ipswich, on the North Shore of Boston. His client was plumbing heir Richard T. Crane, Jr., and his wife Florence, who hired Adler to design what would be the largest house of his career. Adler had known the Crane family for at least twenty-five years. Richard and Florence's nephew, Richard Crane III, was Adler's classmate at Lawrenceville, and in 1916, he designed the Cranes' winter villa on Jekyll Island, Georgia. Now the Cranes called upon him to execute considerably grander plans for their summer home. However, before the English manor

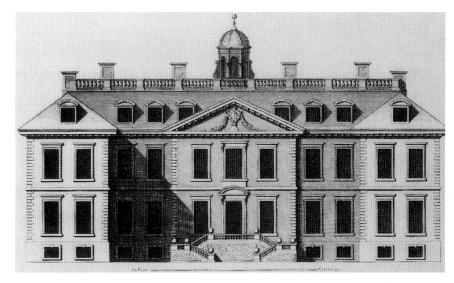

Opposite: Entrance façade

Above: Engraving of Belton House

Gallery

house they commissioned could be built, their existing Italianate house had to be razed.

This house, built in 1911, was designed by the illustrious Boston architectural firm Shepley, Rutan & Coolidge, successors to H. H. Richardson (1838–1886). Shepley, Rutan & Coolidge were well known in Chicago, where they had designed the Art Institute and the Cranes' mansion on Lake Shore Drive (1909).

From the beginning, Mrs. Crane did not like the Ipswich house, claiming that it was too drafty and cold, to cite but one complaint. She wanted the house replaced. Mr. Crane asked his wife to give it ten seasons. If her dissatisfaction persisted, he promised to build her a second house.

She gave it ten summers, and a few more. In 1924, the Cranes asked Adler to draw plans for a new house to be built using the first house's foundation. Adler would also utilize the estate's impressive Italian Renaissance gardens,

including the balustraded terraces and poolside pavilions, which had been designed and executed by the Boston landscape firms of Olmsted Brothers and Arthur Shurcliff. The estate, known as Castle Hill, consisted of nearly 3,500 acres that Crane had purchased over a twenty-year period. At its core was a 165-acre parcel that rose to the property's highest point, from which vantage point the Atlantic Ocean came into spectacular view. Adler's house would be the crowning element to this choice setting of limitless views and brisk ocean breezes.

Seventeenth-century England, particularly the work of Sir Christopher Wren (1632–1723) and the Wren-like Belton House (1689), with its pedimented entrance pavilion, balustraded hip roof, and crowning cupola, served as the inspiration for the Cranes' new house.

Adler chose small Holland brick, whose pink patina softened the great scale of the house.

Against the brick he set limestone trim, which included outlining quoins, a belt course, and a prominent dentil cornice. The Queen Anne–style stone lunette over the front door had its rounded underside intricately carved with images of an angel, a cherub, and decorative floral work—all based on English precedents.

The marble-floored and round-cornered entrance vestibule contained pilaster-framed doorways on all four walls, anchoring the cornice. The doors opened into the women's and men's dressing rooms and the gallery. The composite-order pilasters were crowned by plaster capitals of acanthus leaves, which hinted at the decorative leaf and scroll design of the imposing cornice.

The gallery, with its imported oak parquet-de-Versailles floor, antiqued Georgian paneling, and generous ocean views, formed the nucleus of Castle Hill. Measuring sixty-three by twenty feet, this lobby-like space was the largest room in the house and served not only as a commodious passageway but also as a place where family and guests could relax. The gallery's two sitting areas were grouped around a balanced pair of fireplaces, thus creating intimacy within this vast interior.

Castle Hill also benefited from the work of Abram Poole (1882–1961), who had become a favored artist of East Coast and Midwestern society. Poole embellished the gallery and its adjacent rotunda—a domed vestibule that linked the gallery with the east wing—using earth tones to create a backdrop for the chimney-breast clock and wind-indicator in the gallery and a foundation for the mural in the rotunda. The sole mural of Poole's career, its ceiling portion was modeled after a late-fifteenth-century Italian mural and depicted, among other members of the Crane household, Mr. and Mrs. Crane's children, Florence and Cornelius.

Opposite: Library, Grinling
Gibbons over-mantle

Above: Library

The east wing included the living room and library in addition to a pair of guest suites. The living room, which faced north and east toward the ocean, carried on the English influence with its Georgian paneled walls and period furnishings. As always, Adler arranged the furniture symmetrically, on axis with the central fireplace, and placed, on the same wall, a false double door to balance the room's entrance.

Adjacent to the living room lay the library, a room of consequence in the great houses of England. Adler paid the English tradition a superb tribute when creating the paneled room at Castle Hill—with a little help from his client Marshall Field III. According to a letter in Adler's file, Field referred Edwards and Sons, the London dealer who was the source of the paneling, to Adler. This antique paneling, with its carving by Grinling Gibbons (1648–1720) and pedimented open bookcases, had decked the great library at Cassiobury Park, a historic house in Hertfordshire that was torn down in 1927. When Field, a devoted anglophile, learned of its availability, he knew that Adler would want it. Though Cassiobury was larger and configured differently from Castle Hill (Adler's rectangular-shaped library ended in a spacious bay that took full advantage of the ocean view), Adler was skilled in adaptive reuse. He created a room that retained most of the Cassiobury fittings including the Gibbons carving, a luxuriant swag of oak leaves, fruit, and flowers that seemed to float atop the fireplace over-mantel. On the opposite wall, similar carvings graced the open-pedimented doorways that led outdoors.

Adler also incorporated the original bookcases from Cassiobury Park. Using the historic room for guidance, he lined the paneled walls of his library with these generously proportioned and classically detailed bookcases, allowing

them again to dominate their imposing surroundings.

Adler's strict adherence to symmetry created a house that, despite its grand scale, was eminently livable. When he designed the west wing,
which included the main stair hall and the dining room, he planned it to balance the library
wing. For example, Adler duplicated the
library's footprint in the dining room by positioning this room towards the Atlantic, with a
windowed bay. Although the two rooms were
proportioned similarly, the dining room conveyed a lighter feeling, even with its additional
seven feet of length, primarily because its paneled walls were lacquered pale green. A dentilled band outlined the room's ceiling line as
well as its over-mantel and doorway pediments,
unifying the interior.

Adler skillfully balanced the dining room
with the library, despite the difference in their
length (the extra footage, which he placed at
the entry to the dining room, was necessary
for easy access to the butler's pantry), by separating the additional space with a colonnade.
Thus, he gave the two rooms an illusion of
symmetry.

The additional space in the dining room
was "borrowed" from the main stair hall, with
which Adler aligned the dining room. The
resulting hall still measured twenty-five feet in
length, and in it Adler recreated, albeit on a
larger scale, the staircase from the historic house
at 75 Dean Street, London—once believed to
be the home of artist William Hogarth. When
the townhouse was razed, its interior fittings—
paneling, fireplace mantels and staircase—were
acquired and sold to the Cranes by W. & J.
Sloane in New York. Naturally, Adler and his
clients were elated to obtain these marvelous
materials. In fact, so voluminous was the purchase that it initially had to be stored in the
basement of the Art Institute, according to John
Gregg Allerton, an Adler draftsman who
worked on Castle Hill. Eventually, most of the
contents found their way to Ipswich—but the
staircase was donated to the museum.

The original staircase was too small for
Castle Hill but its detailing could be used, and
Adler created a meticulously accurate rendition.
For example, he replicated the handrail, with its
twist-turned balusters that outlined three sub-
stantial runs of steps that curved around to the

*Opposite, top: Dining room,
view of allée and Atlantic
Ocean*

*Opposite, bottom: Dining
room, view toward stair hall*

Left: Stair hall

*Below: Florence Crane's
sitting room*

View from the allée to
Atlantic Ocean

second floor. From here, the stair hall opened onto a vaulted hallway that ran east to several guest bedrooms and two family suites. The larger of the suites belonged to Mr. and Mrs. Crane. As Adler's files plainly document, 75 Dean Street was again the inspiration: three photographs depict its front and back drawing rooms and small dining room. Adler used the fittings from these rooms—paneling and fireplace mantels—for the Cranes' two bedrooms and Mrs. Crane's sitting room. The paneled sitting room was the largest of the three rooms. Its prominent dentilled cornice and chimney breast, with its pair of towering pilasters and eared mantel surround—were all taken from the townhouse's front drawing room.

Adler gave a dash of eclecticism to this otherwise traditional English house in the two master bathrooms. Mr. Crane was, after all,

president of a prosperous plumbing concern that endeavored to "make America want a better bathroom," and at Castle Hill he wanted luxury in this department. Art deco in style, both bathrooms were furnished with Italian marble and sterling silver fittings.

The living space at Castle Hill extended to a third floor where a chart room occupied the center block of the house. In this spacious room the family, for whom sailing was a favorite pastime, kept its collection of nautical memorabilia. The chart room afforded magnificent views: dormer windows lined two walls, while at the center a circular staircase rose to the house's crowning cupola, which opened onto a surrounding rooftop deck offering a 360-degree panorama.

Another breathtaking sight was the 160-foot-wide allée of grass that undulated, from the terrace façade towards the Atlantic Ocean, half a

mile away. Although Arthur Shurcliff planned this vista in 1914, its basic concept, which linked the house with the distant ocean, closely resembled Adler's garden design for the Pike house. This coincidence was fortuitous, because Adler had his own opinions about landscaping and could be masterful in asserting them. With the landscape plan already in place, Adler put his mind to creating a terrace façade that was not dwarfed by the vista it overlooked: the projecting wings of the library and dining room balanced the house's principal block in a triumph of massing.

The Crane house was completed in 1928; Richard Crane died suddenly, three years later, at the age of fifty-eight. His widow and their two children continued to summer at Castle Hill. By the mid-1940s, Florence Crane had begun to plan for the future of her estate by donating one thousand acres of her property to the Trustees of Reservations, a Massachusetts land conservation society. At her death in 1949, additional acreage also passed to the Trustees, along with the house and its dependent buildings, including a pair of Adler-designed gatehouses. One year after Mrs. Crane's death, the interior furnishings and art were auctioned on the premises over a three-day period by New York's Parke-Bernet Galleries. The catalogue, 225 pages long, noted: "The great mansion 'Castle Hill' was designed for Mrs. Richard Crane by David Adler, one of America's most noted domestic architects, who also carried out the detail of the interior and was responsible for the selection of the furniture and furnishings, which reflect his sensitive and conservative taste."

Today, Castle Hill and its surrounding property, including Crane's Beach, are open to the public, and the estate hosts numerous public and private events each year.

View from the allée to house

Top: Mill Road Farm, aerial view

Above: Photograph of Norman farmhouse in Adler files

Opposite: Approach to the house

Mr. and Mrs. Albert D. Lasker

Everett, Illinois, 1925
Interiors with Frances Elkins
Standing

Designing Castle Hill would have been formidable to most architects, but Adler accepted the commission at a time when he was also working on an ambitious project on Chicago's North Shore for advertising entrepreneur Albert D. Lasker. Lasker, his wife Flora, and their three children, Mary, Edward, and Frances, lived in a townhouse on Chicago's Gold Coast and summered on the North Shore. Chicago architect Samuel Marx (1885–1964) designed their first country house in Glencoe in 1912. The house edged the golf course at the Lake Shore Country Club, allowing Lasker easy access to one of his favorite sports.

As early as 1917, Lasker asked Adler to design a French chateau to be built overlooking the lake in the neighboring town of Highland

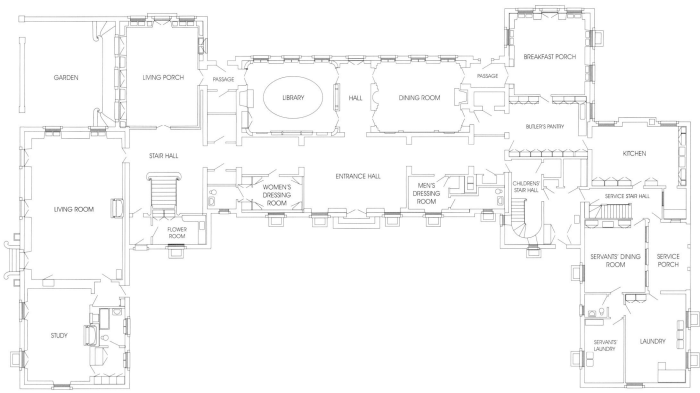

GARDEN

LIVING PORCH

PASSAGE

LIBRARY

HALL

DINING ROOM

PASSAGE

BREAKFAST PORCH

BUTLER'S PANTRY

KITCHEN

STAIR HALL

ENTRANCE HALL

WOMEN'S DRESSING ROOM

MEN'S DRESSING ROOM

CHILDRENS STAIR HALL

SERVICE STAIR HALL

LIVING ROOM

FLOWER ROOM

SERVANTS' DINING ROOM

SERVICE PORCH

STUDY

SERVANTS' LAUNDRY

LAUNDRY

Park. The house, a mansard-roofed building, was a variation on Adler's earlier house for the Pooles, again based on the Hôtel Biron, especially in the use of enfilade. Other elements from the source were a stone-and-marble-checkered entrance hall, a stone staircase, and the rounded bays at the rear of the house.

Adler designed six other buildings for the Lasker property in addition: a pair of gate lodges, a garage and stable, a greenhouse, and a poultry house. The commission did not come to fruition; however, it foreshadowed the even grander plans that Lasker had for a property that he soon purchased near Lake Forest. During the early 1920s, in his quest to create the quintessential estate (one that *Country Life* termed, in 1941, "An American Chantilly"), Lasker began acquiring several contiguous properties in Everett, Illinois, a bucolic community west of Lake Forest. Eventually his property, which included a working farm, totaled nearly five hundred acres. The focal point of this new summer place, to be called Mill Road Farm or just "the Farm," would be its Adler-designed house in the style of a seventeenth-century French manor, with one hundred acres of formally landscaped gardens and a private eighteen-hole golf course that cost a million dollars.

Construction of Mill Road Farm took three years, beginning in 1925. Coordinating the various facets of the estate, including the layout of its roads, gardens, golf course, and twenty-six dependent buildings, required considerable planning.

The entrance to the estate was off Old Mill Road, the property's southernmost boundary. From the gate lodge, the tree-lined drive continued north, then curved to the west, meeting a straightaway to the walled forecourt of the house. Hedges immaculately trimmed in a geometric pattern embraced the final leg of the half-mile drive and hinted at the perfectionism that awaited beyond.

Informality and comfort were important to Lasker. The entrance to the forecourt was centered in a white picket fence balanced by a pair of octagonal colombiers, but the capacious and imposing size of the house was not apparent. U-shaped, the house consisted of a center block balanced by twin mansard-roofed wings. A tall pitched roof, with a pair of oeil-de-boeuf

dormers, crowned the center block and proclaimed the French provincial origin of Adler's design. The roof's clay-tiled surface, shaded in colors of brown and red, contrasted with the whitewashed brick façade, battleship-gray shutters, and turkey-red awnings.

A marquee in wrought iron and glass sheltered the front door, which opened into a spacious, rectangular entrance hall. Paved in brick red quarry tile, the beamed hall connected to hallways that ran west to the principal terrace, south to the main stair hall, and north to the service wing. Closest to the entrance hall was the terrace, but between the stair hall and service wing was an expanse of over eighty feet—the first indication of the house's size—which Adler segmented with a succession of evenly spaced archways that visually reduced the distance.

In addition to the entrance hall and its ancillary hallways, the center block of the house contained the women's and men's dressing rooms, which overlooked the entrance forecourt, the library, and the dining room. Situated on opposite sides of the terrace doorway, the library and dining room balanced one another.

The interiors of the Lasker house received a good deal of attention and input from Flora Lasker, who turned to Frances Elkins, who had already worked on the Laskers' Glencoe house. However, when it came to decorating the estate's guest house, an old, remodeled farm building, Flora Lasker handled the task herself. She loved antiques, and the guest house was home to her Early American treasures.

Elkins searched diligently—and with success—in France for the interiors of the main house, finding the antique wallpaper that set the tone of the dining room in shades of turquoise and pale brown. The empire-style paper depicted the muses of Greek mythology, appropriate accents to Adler's classically detailed moldings and paneled over-mantel, which framed a carving of Louis XIV.

Across the hall, the library conveyed a completely different feeling from the dining room, despite their identical proportions. The library's oval-domed ceiling and rounded corners softened the interior and created seamless transitions between the book-lined walls. Even the doors were fronted with rows of leather bind-

ings to simulate additional bookshelves. Contrasting colors were also integral to the atmosphere: canary yellow walls complemented the heavy earth tones of the leather and the antique furniture.

Linked by a small hallway to the library was the living porch. Called the "Blue Room" because of the periwinkle blue glaze of its herringbone tile, its mullioned windows overlooked Flora Lasker's intimate garden, the west lawn, and the principal terrace of the house. A beamed ceiling and French provincial furnishings gave the room a homey, country look.

The living porch also opened into the main stair hall, which joined the first and second floors and connected the first-floor rooms, rendering an expansive floor plan efficient and eminently livable. One archway in the hall connected with the entrance hall, while a doorway led to the drawing room.

Opposite: Entrance hall

Top: Dining room

Above: Library

The drawing room dominated the south wing. It was a grand salon in the truest sense, with eighteenth-century pine paneling and antique parquet-de-Versailles floor hosting Elkins's selection of Louis XV–style chairs, painted stools, and a bombé commode. (Plank flooring was used at first, but when the brother-and-sister team found parquet in France; the entire floor was redone.) The drawing room, twenty-four by thirty-six feet, accommodated several seating areas, each planned around the room's brown marble fireplace mantel. Through the French windows could be seen Flora Lasker's garden, and to the south, towards the swimming pool and the distant farm buildings, a vista of the garden allée. A private study adjoined the drawing room—the "most comfortable room in the whole house," according to Cyrill Tregillus, Lasker's estate manager. The second floor of the house, reached by the main staircase, utilized the full footage of the downstairs. The staircase itself was dramatic: beginning with a straight run of steps to a landing, the staircase then diverged into two flights that curved around from each side of the landing to the second-floor stair hall.

On the second floor, the stair hall linked the rooms. To the south, above the drawing room and study, was the men's wing, containing Edward's bedroom and his father's master suite—a bedroom, dressing room, and bath. Albert Lasker's bedroom, with its wood paneling, antique parquetry, and a fireplace precisely centered on the north wall, was earthy and masculine. To balance the entrance to the dressing room, Adler added a false door on an adjacent wall. Despite the door's lack of utility, it opened—and it was stamped in two places on its unfinished side, "Made in France."

Flora Lasker's suite, located in the house's center block, was even more luxurious than her husband's. In the bedroom a soft ivory hue glazed the paneled walls whose contour included a pair of rounded corners. Mullioned windows on three sides of the bedroom admitted generous views; one full-length window opened to a verandah that faced the golf course. But the boudoir was the most elegant room. Connected to the bedroom via the dressing room, it had unique, curved corners and exquisite wallpaper panels in exotic colors—shades of celadon green, sand, and ivory—framed by pan-

Opposite: Living room

View of terrace façade facing golf course

eled walls. Also incorporated in the paneling were four recessed cases that displayed Flora Lasker's collection of objets d'art. One pair of these cases lay flat against one wall, while the other two were shaped by the S-curve of the corners, which they balanced.

Outside the boudoir a long hallway served all the rooms within the center block of the house: a large sitting room, two guest rooms, and Frances Lasker's bedroom. The sitting room, set exactly over the entrance hall below, was the core of the second-floor plan.

A house of this magnitude required a tremendous staff. For them, Adler provided nine servants' bedrooms in the north wing and more in other buildings on the estate; Lasker's staff often numbered as many as fifty.

Much attention and care was devoted to the grounds of Mill Road Farm. Sweeping towards the golf course from the symmetrical rear elevation of the house, was a vast lawn, which, along with the estate's numerous gardens and six miles of clipped hedges, required a phalanx of gardeners. There was a separate

crew for the golf course and even a man who brushed the morning dew off the lawn!

Originally, Louise Hubbard (1887–1932), a landscape designer from the North Shore, had worked on the ground plan for "the Farm," but in 1931 Lasker decided to replace her. New York landscape architect James Greenleaf (1857–1933) made various changes, including the realignment of the elms and shrubs along the main drive as well as reconfiguring several vistas on the estate.

Adler's design for the dependencies on the Lasker estate followed suit with the main house. Especially picturesque were the twin dollhouse-like bathhouses—small whitewashed brick buildings with mansard roofs—that balanced the end of the drawing room allée, though trees screened them from the main house. A terraced lawn led down to the pool area, juxtaposing the swimming pool and bathhouses against the main house's south wing, one of the most effective vistas of Adler's career.

Adler designed a third building, the pavilion, for the west end of the pool. Although

*Living room wing,
facing garden allée
and swimmng pool*

*Overleaf: View from
swimming pool toward house*

crescent-shaped and larger than the bathhouses, it was also whitewashed brick with a mansard roof. Inside was a central lounge whose two walls of tall French windows faced the pool and the nearby topiary garden. In this engaging setting, gourmet lunches were served daily. Included was dessert from the lounge's built-in ice cream bar.

The sunken topiary garden, west of the pavilion, was cultivated long before the building was added. The half-acre fantasy garden was the pet project of head gardener Robert Brydon. Here, using Chinese elms, birds, love seats, and geometric configurations were trimmed into being.

Another popular attraction of Mill Road Farm was the recreation building, sited northeast of the main house, off the entrance drive. It was an enlarged version of the bathhouses built during the early 1930s. Lasker enjoyed one of his favorite pastimes here: movies. Each week, three first-run films were screened for family, friends, and members of the household staff (including bodyguards in the era of kid-nappings), who joined Lasker in the two dozen comfortable lounge chairs upholstered in a dark-blue resist. The building was also used for buffet parties; tables and ballroom chairs replaced the lounge chairs, and from the stage, where the projection screen was positioned for the screenings, a band serenaded the guests.

The largest expanse of landscaped acreage at Mill Road Farm stretched north of the main drive and due east of the forecourt. The first division consisted of fruit orchards: pear, apple, plum, and cherry, all planted in rows around two tennis courts. The courts themselves were sited on axis with the monumental eight-car garage at the opposite end of the garden. Together, the tennis courts and the garage anchored a garden allée that ran the entire landscaped distance.

Balancing the allée were a pair of English border gardens, bursting with a profusion of color and texture. The flower beds rested against a wall of meticulously trimmed hedges, which gave structure and height to the garden and screened the cutting gardens that proceeded in

Topiary garden

unison with the flower beds. A dividing allée running east-west opened into these interior gardens, revealing further the artistry and painstaking detail that defined Mill Road Farm. The plantings and beds, in quadrants, were outlined by low privet hedges.

The eastern end of the cross allée also led to the brick potting house, with its tall pitched roof, and the three greenhouses, which together formed a U. The greenhouses were in constant use, especially for the cultivation of Belgian grapes, orchids, and—most important—Lasker's experimental freeze-resistant chrysanthemums. Naturally, the flower room in the main house was kept well supplied.

Albert Lasker was proud of his farm, which he operated as a business. Most of the buildings belonged to the original farm and included a substantial whitewashed red brick barn, which Lasker renovated at a cost of seventy-five thousand dollars. Lasker raised Guernsey cows and,

in an Adler-designed poultry house, chickens. Each week, the resulting eggs, milk, and cream were sold at a nearby market.

Mill Road Farm abounded with family and friends. Albert and Flora Lasker encouraged their children to have guests, and Lasker himself loved to hold golf outings, hosting amateur players as well as professionals, captains of industry, and presidents.

Flora Lasker's time at Mill Road Farm was limited to nine seasons: she died suddenly in December 1936 while on a trip to New York. The family continued in residence for the following three summers, but by the end of 1939 Lasker had decided to give the estate to the University of Chicago. He had been on their board for several years and thought that the Farm would be an ideal location for botanical research and experimentation. After all, Lasker himself had set up a plot of experimental greens for the United States Golf Association—

View from garden allée toward garage

not to mention the freeze-resistant chrysanthemums. A stipulation of accepting the gift was that the university retain the property for at least two years.

During the short time that the University of Chicago owned Mill Road Farm, the gardens were opened to the public. Even the house was open to tourists—once.

Lasker, who was then living in New York with his third wife, Mary, also rented the house for part of the summers of 1940 and 1941. Although their time at the Farm together was brief, it left a lasting impression on Mary Lasker. The philanthropist renowned for her and her husband's dedication to medical research and urban beautification recalled some forty years later that she enjoyed living there "immensely." Mary Lasker did not know David Adler, but she thought him to be "the best domestic architect of this country in this century."

By 1942 maintaining Mill Road Farm had become a financial drain for the university and it began selling off the acreage for the construction of new houses. Fortunately, several of the outbuildings were converted into individual houses: the garage, recreation building, and potting house remain. The main house was sold. One of its early owners was architect Jerome Cerny, who had been a draftsman in Adler's office during the design of Mill Road Farm and loved the house before the plans ever left the office. He purchased the house in 1945, divided its vast interior into three sections, and lived with his family at the south end of the house, while renting the remaining sections to other families. After Cerny died in 1970, the house returned to the market; passing into the hands of a succession of caring owners whose intent was to restore the house to a single-family residence. This has been accomplished, albeit on only eight acres.

Entrance façade

Mr. and Mrs. William McCormick Blair

Lake Bluff, Illinois, 1926
Standing

Adler's next commission on the North Shore was for his close friend William McCormick Blair and his wife Helen, both descendants of distinguished families of Chicago. Blair was Adler's financial advisor and the trustee of his estate.

It was Helen Blair's appreciation for Early American architecture that most influenced Adler's design for their country house. To shape and clarify their ideas and tastes, the Blairs motored along the East Coast with Adler, visiting the Blairs' friends J. Watson Webb and his wife Electra at their estate in Old Westbury, Long Island, as well as the Webbs' farm in Shelburne, Vermont. (Years later the Webbs founded the Shelburne Museum, which housed their collection of Early Americana.)

The Blairs' property in Lake Bluff was nestled into the northeast corner of a 270-acre dairy farm, called Crab Tree Farm. Blair purchased the wooded eleven-acre parcel that overlooked Lake Michigan during the late 1920s from Grace Durand, proprietor of the farm. Soon after the purchase, Blair and his son Edward accompanied Adler as he staked the property for the house along the estate's northeast boundary.

The Blairs' house demonstrates Adler's versatility. Although the Early American style was not new to Adler—he had used it in Shore Acres (1923), an intimate golf club that was just north of Crab Tree Farm—his plan for the Blairs was uncharacteristically asymmetrical. It was not this way at first, though. According to Henry O. Milliken (1884–1945), a classmate of Adler at Princeton who joined Adler and Work

Entrance pavilion

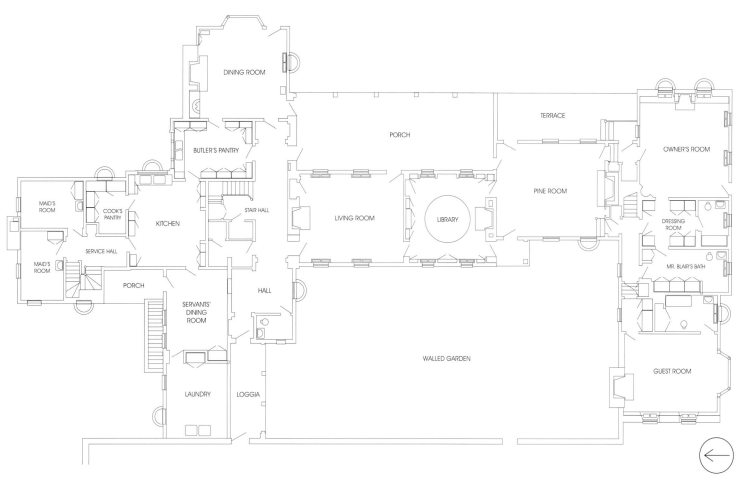

for several years before he established his own firm in New York, the original sketch for the house combined French and Greek revival styles and consisted of a center block that was balanced by a pair of identical wings. (Milliken retained Adler's original sketch, which he later donated to the Cooper-Hewitt Museum in Manhattan.)

The final design, which suited the Blairs' taste and the village setting of Crab Tree Farm, placed the house at the secluded end of a private drive that passed through the farm. Once completed, the house looked as if it had always been there; the same held true for the service quadrangle, which preceded the house along the drive. The irregular massing of colonial architecture, whereby a house grows larger over time, dictated Adler's design. Although the house was built all at once, Adler's adaptation flawlessly suggested an organic progression of growth from the principal block, shingled and gambrel-roofed, to the appended wings.

The wings that projected from the north end of the house into the gravel forecourt contained the entrance pavilion. Gable-fronted and adroitly scaled, the pavilion was faced with a combination of fieldstone and hand-split shingles. Also adding texture to the façade was the detailing of its entrance door and outlining surround. For example, incised chevrons in white patterned the door's jet-black panels, while fluting defined the flanking pair of pilasters.

The entrance pavilion recalled the Pike house, which was also fronted by a walled garden. Adler reapplied the proven design and gave the entrance an arcaded loggia that overlooked the garden and led to the main doorway.

The interior plan of the Blair house was designed to take full advantage of its enviable setting. The house was only one room deep, so its principal rooms offered unobstructed views of both Lake Michigan and the walled garden. To achieve the multiple exposure, Adler omitted the customary central gallery from his first-floor plan, using instead the sequence of living room, library, and sitting room (the "Pine Room") to link the north and south wings. However, there was a principal hall in the north wing that connected, in its easterly span, the dining room, living room, living porch, main stair hall and service wing. Particularly notable was the pine paneled hall, with its pilaster-sup-ported archways and wainscoting following colonial precedents. Adler detailed the hall innovatively to take into account the Blairs' extensive collection of Currier and Ives prints: the framed prints were set flush into recessed openings into the paneling.

The dining room was modeled on the Hewlett Room in the American Wing at the Metropolitan Museum of Art in New York. Adler followed closely the details of this historic eighteenth-century room. He duplicated the projecting cornice and fireplace wall, with its Delft-tiled fireplace surround, double-capped fluted pilasters, and a built-in shell cupboard—but in Adler's version, the mantel is centered and has a second, balancing shell cupboard. Adler added a bay window to the room to give a view of Lake Michigan.

The comfortable and unassuming decor was created by Helen Blair. According to Dorothy Mosiman, Mr. Blair's executive assistant for many years, Mrs. Blair was a talented interior designer who excelled under David Adler's tutelage. She selected eighteenth- and nineteenth-century furniture for her classically detailed rooms. In the living room, English pieces mixed well with Adler's Georgian paneling that was lightened with cream paint. Nineteenth-century chintz curtains with a green-and-white floral pattern softened the interior and related it to the lakeside living porch and the walled garden outdoors, which could be seen through mullioned windows and Dutch doorways.

The fifteen-foot-square library was paneled, its classical details—straight-edged panels and arched openings—accentuated by an unusual shade of terra cotta. Adler also designed the square area rug, an arrangement of bold yellow stars on a brown background; at its center a circular design mirrored the shape of the cove ceiling.

Although Adler created most of the Blair interiors, he also welcomed into his plan a period room that came intact from an eighteenth-century Virginia house. It formed the sitting room—called the "Pine Room" for its natural-colored paneled walls and dentilled cornice—and it fit Adler's colonial scheme comfortably. The third and largest of the principal rooms, it was floored in random-width oak plank. Like the living room and library, it brought the outdoors inside with tall mullioned windows and a pair of

Opposite: Entrance hall, view toward dining room

Dining room

Right: Photograph of Hewlett Room, Metropolitan Museum of Art in Adler files. The Delft tile does not appear in this photograph.

Opposite: Library

The Pine Room.
Greek-revival summerhouse
is seen in the distance

View of garden

turned spindles, matched on its wainscoted inner wall by a series of pilasters that created a faux railing.

The Blair living porch was one of Adler's most successful. Sited along the eastern edge of the house's main block, it captured a sweeping expanse of Lake Michigan. The shingled side of the main block and its shuttered windows served as the backdrop for the porch. The living room and library windows and the doorways that opened into the living room, dining room, and sitting room all opened onto the porch, thus linking those rooms with the outside.

A walled garden adjoined the living room, library, and sitting room. Designed by landscape architect Ellen Biddle Shipman (1869–1950), the parterred garden's flower beds were outlined with boxwood, and brick walkways offered a path through beds of roses. Flowering pear trees stood sentry against the house.

The allée from the house to the summerhouse related the house and its dependent buildings. Though the summerhouse, with its pedimented roofline and columned front, was the focal point of the allée; it foreshadowed the extensive service quadrangle to its south. Closest to this pavilion was the tennis house with an indoor court, added a few years after completion of the main house in a collaboration between Adler and James W. O'Connor (1876–1952) of New York. O'Connor, an architect who enjoyed a reputation on par with Adler's, was known especially for the recreational buildings or "playhouses" that he designed for East Coast society—which included the Webbs, at their Long Island estate. Here, again, the Blairs looked to their friends for advice.

Adler and O'Connor designed a Georgian building whose detailing included quoins, paneled shutters, and a balustraded roofline. The tennis building also housed a lounge, a pair of dressing rooms, and a small kitchen. Its entrance, like that of the main house, was from the west through an arcaded loggia. Inside, knotty pine paneled the central lounge, whose French doors opened to the court. There, natural light flooded the space through a towering pitched glass roof. A wainscoting of ivy and its offspring of topiary-like figures—spread eagles and roosters—covered the court's walls. Building the Blair tennis house came at a good time for Adler. The knowledge that he absorbed

windowed paneled doors that opened on opposite sides of the room onto a lakeside terrace and the walled garden, providing an expansive vista from Lake Michigan in the east to, west of the main house, a Greek-revival summerhouse nestled in the woods at the end of a broad allée.

The Pine Room also influenced Adler's plan for the south wing. Because the room included a few steps on its fireplace wall, which led to the master suite, it was necessary to elevate the master bedroom suite above the main floor. This slight elevation gave greater privacy to the suite, since it shared a hall with a guest room, a few steps down, at ground level.

Another guest room was located on the second floor, which also held the bedrooms for the Blair children and their governess. These bedrooms could be reached by either the main staircase or an auxiliary staircase from the master bedroom wing.

The main staircase, crowned by an oval skylight, had a colonial-style balustrade of hand-

Tennis court

from James O'Connor in this first design served him well for a major commission that soon followed: a tennis house for Mr. and Mrs. Kersey Coates Reed in Lake Forest.

To the west and directly in line with the tennis house and its gravel forecourt were the requisite planting garden and two buildings that were part of the service group's quadrangular plan—the greenhouse and the potting shed. Adjacent to the potting shed was the gardener's cottage which, along with the garage-laundry building, framed the entrance to the quadrangle's gravel courtyard. Particularly innovative was the design of the garage. Because the building edged the drive to the main house, Adler modeled its roadside elevation after an early colonial house, perpetuating the village feeling and concealing any indication of the building's actual use. The building featured a white clapboard façade with an overhanging second floor housing additional staff quarters. Inside the quadrangle, Adler faced his colonial house with

three garage doors whose arched configuration was replicated on two shelter sheds. One shed completed the quadrangle, while the other anchored the main house's entrance forecourt.

William Blair summered at his Lake Bluff house throughout his life. Even during the winter, he and his wife, who died ten years before he did, would stay in their tennis house when they visited from Chicago on weekends. By 1952, Blair had purchased the remainder of Crab Tree Farm from Grace Durand. Soon after, his son Edward built a house on the property, also overlooking Lake Michigan.

William Blair died in 1982, in his late nineties, and his death represented the passing of a generation of Chicago aristocracy. Crab Tree Farm passed into the hands of a family whose passion and interest sustained David Adler's memory: the main house, its dependencies, and the gardens and grounds have all been painstakingly restored. Even the farm has been preserved, as has the estate's coveted privacy.

Mr. and Mrs. William E. Clow, Jr.

Lake Forest, Illinois, 1927
Standing

Adler's second house for the Clows

Adler's next commission in Lake Forest came from Isabelle and William Clow, Jr. The Clows had been among the first clients of the Adler-Dangler office; in 1913 Adler designed for them in Lake Forest a small English regency house, a singular block of perfect symmetry accentuated by a veneer of yellow stucco and simple late Georgian detailing—a pedimented entrance with fanlight, dentilled cornice, and panelled shutters. The inside was compact: on the first floor a center hall divided the space in half. On the right were a living room and its connecting living porch, while the dining room, serving pantry, and kitchen balanced them on the opposite side of the hall. A staircase from the hall led upstairs to four family bedrooms, two baths, and the maids' quarters. A little gem, this house was prelude to Adler's sec-

ond and much larger commission for the Clows, completed fourteen years later on a nearby site.

The second Clow house was also Adler's only built essay in "modern" design. Adler greatly admired the work of Mies van der Rohe (1886–1969). The Clow house was directly influenced by the Viennese designer Josef Hoffmann (1870–1956), though the connection did not come to light until the early 1990s, when Christian Witt-Dorring, a visiting curator from the Austrian Museum of Applied Arts in Vienna, attended a luncheon held at the Clow house. After touring the house, Witt-Dorring told the current owners, Morris and Jane Weeden, that their house was in Vienna. The Weedens were intrigued, and Witt-Dorring arranged for them to visit Hoffmann's Villa Primavesi (1913).

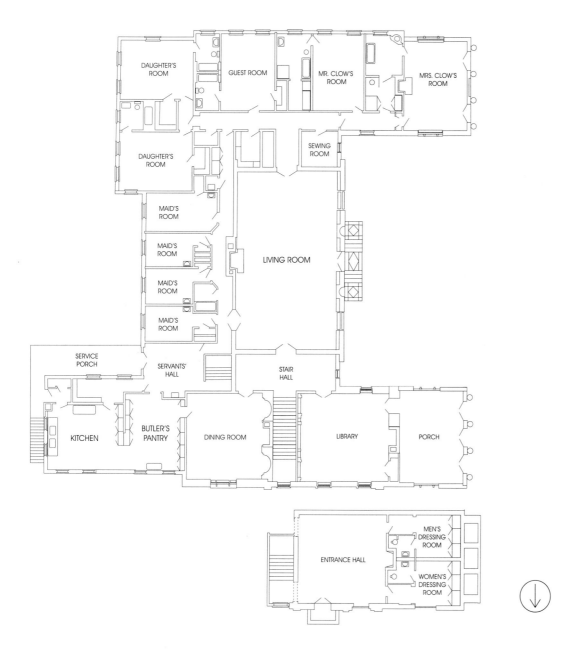

The similarities were unmistakeable: Jane Weeden felt the familiarity of the European *piano nobile*, the formal rooms located on the second floor, and the expansiveness of the staircase leading to it. Most striking, however, was the Primavesi garden teahouse and accompanying wooden, cagelike wall identical to the wall of the Clow forecourt. Adler's version consisted of a series of tall iron bars, evenly spaced in groupings of six, set into a framework of stucco. A horizontal bar running through the center of the wall embraced a delicate touch of decorative ironwork, which was repeated in the middle of each section. Several photographs of the villa are in Adler's file; clearly he was inspired by Hoffmann's design.

The Hoffmann teahouse, with its pedimented roofline and supporting piers, also echoed in Adler's design for the projecting center section of the Clow façade and the twin temple-like pavilions of the garden elevation, though the federal and Greek revival elements of these pavilions is more consistent with Adler's style. (They also foreshadow two purely classical designs he would create in the early 1930s: the Lester Armour house and the Edison Dick house, both on Chicago's North Shore.)

The Clow house had the symmetrical balance typical of a David Adler design. Its façade of whitewashed brick was set below the umbrella of an expansive metal roof. A smaller pediment supported by fluted pilasters framed the brilliant red front door that opened from the pebbled forecourt into the entrance hall.

With its cove molding and a black terrazzo floor, the square entrance hall established the

Photograph of
Villa Primavesi teahouse
in Adler files

Adler's first house for the
Clows in Lake Forest

Entrance hall in second house for the Clows

tone of the interior. A pair of doors flanking a fireplace opened into identical dressing rooms. Directly across from the women's dressing room, an archway led to the staircase, which rose to the upstairs stair hall with its vaulted ceiling and diamond-patterned black marble floor. Off it were the library, dining room, and living room.

The paneled Georgian library with its cove ceiling was the only traditional room in the house. Pilasters, moldings, and trim highlighted the doorways and built-in bookcases and concealed the radiators installed below each of the room's three windows. A connecting garden room stepped down a short distance to the garden, elevated by truckloads of fill to equalize it with the main floor of the house.

In contrast to the library, the dining room at the opposite end of the stair hall was pure art deco. Its prominent ceiling of graduated levels and a pair of tall niches on the fireplace wall were outlined in a stepped border. The walls were covered in split-straw marquetry, custom-made for the room by Parisian designer Adolphe Chanaux (1887–1965), who became the partner of Jean-Michel Frank. A handsome, richly stained wooden floor was a suitable counterpoint to Isabelle Clow's pewter furniture, made to order in Sweden. Isabelle Clow was a passionate collector who acquired modern furnishings and works of art from several countries. Upon completion, the dining table had been displayed in a Stockholm museum;

though the Swedish government requested that it remain there permanently, the table eventually reached its intended destination.

The library and dining room, both generous in proportions, were modest compared to the living room. Occupying the heart of the house across the stair hall, it was monumental. A set of towering, concentrically paneled doors in white lacquer announced the room, whose commanding presence was on par with the palatial spaces in Adler's largest commissions. Crowned by an imposing cove ceiling of double height, the gallery-like room enjoyed a generous view of the garden through three sets of windows, the center pair functioning as French doors. On the opposite wall, natural light from the east filtered through a pair of balancing roundels placed below the cove. Light sparkled continuously in the room's twin crystal and amethyst chandeliers. The walls were covered in gray French raw silk, providing a muted textured palette for Isabelle Clow's collection of contemporary furnishings and art; the floor was black herringbone parquetry. Adler placed three additional pairs of lacquered doors along the south and east walls: two served the adjoining family and servants' hallways, while the third, a false doorway, maintained symmetry.

The doors to the family quarters opened onto a vaulted hall that led to the Clows' separate master suites, three additional bedrooms, and the sewing and linen rooms. In the guest bedroom twin beds were suspended slightly above the floor, the corners of their wood frames attached to chains anchored in the ceiling. In Mrs. Clow's suite, over-pediments supported by rounded pilasters framed a pair of doorways, emphasizing the room's identity as the balancing pavilion to the library's garden room. The crown molding resembled that of the dining room; Adler liked consistency and employed the same detailing in all five bedrooms. Mrs. Clow's bath was lavishly appointed in marble. Dark black-and-green compass designs dotted the marble floor, their boldness

Opposite: Living room

contrasting with the stone's natural veined patterning in shades of aubergine and off-white.

Mrs. Clow's suite also opened onto the garden. From here, looking back at the house, the building formed a U composed of the twin pavilions, with their black columns, and the living room core of the house. Greek fretwork grilles ran atop the outside wall of the living room and twin neoclassical arched niches were placed between the living room windows. An outlining flagstone walkway delineated the garden and its slightly depressed center lawn.

At the edge of the property, a handsome stuccoed wall overlooked Green Bay Road. On the garden side, a series of pedestals and enjoining bench seating was incorporated into the wall. Imposing black iron Swedish urns, set atop the pedestals and visible from the road, allowed the passerby but a hint of grandeur, never revealing that the wall concealed a garden that was elevated substantially above street level.

Adler revisited the Clow house two decades after its completion, when Leola Stanton Armour purchased it in 1949. Leola Armour had already built and furnished one Adler house, in Lake Bluff in 1931, with her former husband Lester. When they divorced, she searched for a house large enough to accommodate her possessions. The Clow house fit the bill. Before Leola Armour moved into her new house she naturally turned to David Adler for assistance; they were good friends. Adler helped her choose a location in the library for the large breakfront that had come from the Lake Bluff house: a center section holding a built-in bookcase was removed, creating the appropriate home for this handsome piece of furniture. The alteration was consistent with the tone of the library and its traditional feeling, but would have been distinctly out of touch with the other principal rooms in the house—the dining room and the living room.

The Clow commission was one of the last houses executed during the association of Adler and Work. When Adler received his license in 1929, he had built thirty-three houses. The next phase of his career would produce several important buildings.

*Leola Armour's mirrored
dressing room, detail*

PART III

ADLER'S ECLECTIC CLASSICISM
1929–1935

The Golden Era of the American Great House

Mrs. Celia Tobin Clark

Hillsborough, California, 1929
Standing

Adler's commission for Celia Tobin Clark in Hillsborough, California, an affluent neighborhood south of San Francisco, marked the beginning of his solo career. Initially, Celia Clark commissioned her friend, nationally known San Francisco architect Arthur Brown, Jr. (1874–1957; designer of San Francisco's City Hall and War Memorial Opera House) to design the house that would sit on her El Palomar property. Brown had already designed a Mediterranean villa for Celia Clark in Pebble Beach in the 1920s.

Celia Clark was heiress to the Hibernia banking fortune, and had recently divorced her husband, Charles Clark. In the divorce settlement she received the house, El Palomar, where they had lived with their four children, and its grounds, nearly five hundred acres of prime hillside property. El Palomar was a large Georgian revival house that stood at the eastern edge of the property, too close to the busy El Camino Real to suit Celia Clark. She relished her privacy and decided to move her family further up the hill.

Celia Clark sold one hundred acres to the neighboring St. Matthew's Catholic Church (eventually the house was also deeded to the church and was converted into a parish school). She then hired Arthur Brown, who envisioned a large French chateau, three stories tall, rising imposingly from the top of the hill—the opposite of what his client had in mind. Celia Clark wanted an English house that disappeared into the landscape, like those she had seen in the Cotswolds on visits to England with her family. Celia Clark knew of David Adler through the Dillinghams, good friends of her brother, Richard Tobin, and chose Adler to create what became known as House-on-Hill.

Mrs. Clark gave a great deal of thought to ways of improving the property and creating an idyllic setting for the new house. As early as 1921, she had begun transplanting full-grown trees from Monterey; she moved entire oak groves and even imported a stone top pine tree from Italy. No expense was spared.

Entrance façade

111

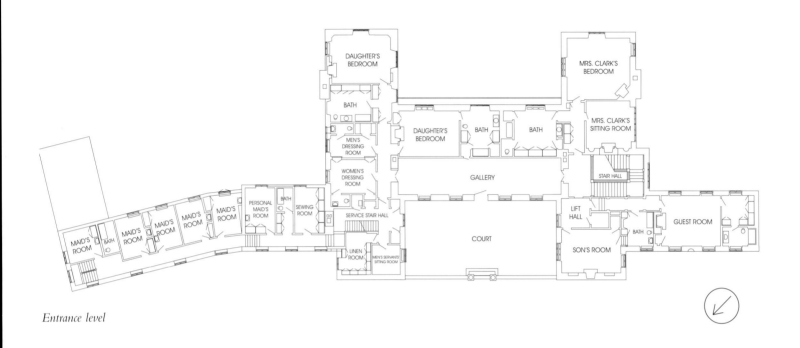

Entrance level

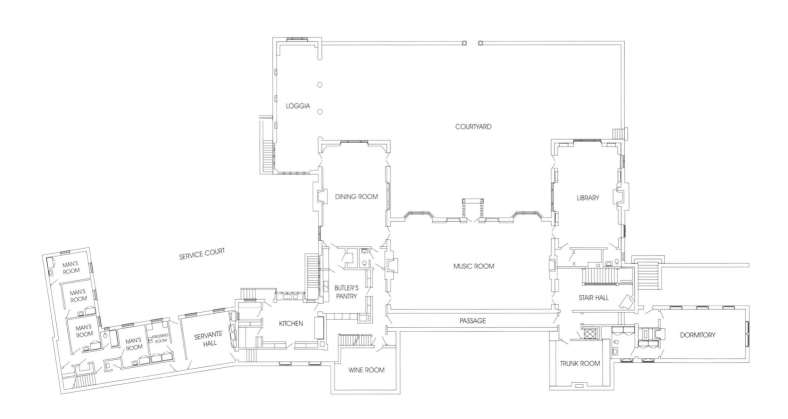

Terrace façade

Construction was completed in several stages. First to be built, on the lower part of the estate, set back from the eucalyptus-lined entrance drive that led from Alameda de las Pulgas, were a thirteen-bay carriage house, servants' cottage, and guest cottage, where the family lived while the main house was being built.

This three-building complex and the next-to-be-built stables, which stood across the drive as balance to the carriage house, guarded the drive at the start of its sinuous climb up the hill toward the main house.

House-on-Hill was sheltered from sight until one was almost at the front door. Celia Clark wanted an inconspicuous façade, and Adler delivered. Not until the road neared the almost perfectly square entrance forecourt and its balancing pair of monumental, globe-capped pillars in Carmel stone did sight of the house appear. The handsomely textured honey-colored stone—reminiscent of the Cotswolds—

was unimposing. Nestled into the hillside, overlooking rolling hills and winding canyons, at its entrance forecourt House-on-Hill appeared to be only one and a half stories.

The house was built on an H-plan, and its full magnitude became apparent only at the back, from the south terrace, where the Elizabethan half-timbered façade rose majestically, as if it grew from the landscape. It offered complete privacy and solitude; from it, Celia Clark would never see another house.

Celia Clark's daughter, Agnes Albert, said that living at House-on-Hill was like being on an island. From the south terrace nothing could be seen except the natural surroundings of this magnificent property. The terrace faced an oak-studded hill that rose from an encircling canyon. The view back toward the house, where Adler's most complex and impressive façade came into view, was equally spectacular. On the first floor leaded glass windows in the library, music room, and dining room lay set into a wall

Reception gallery, view toward main stair hall

Below: Library

Opposite: Library, Grinling Gibbons over-mantel

of Carmel stone that gave the house soft and mellow tones and complemented the half-timbering of the façade.

Evenly spaced oak timbers were positioned around sections of brick nogging laid meticulously in varied patterns. The effect was a compelling but not busy façade. The main block was divided into three even sections, with a six-part leaded glass window centered on each section on the second floor. Above these windows three gabled dormers crowned a steep roofline.

Inside the Clark house, the initial floor plan gave no indication of the house's vast dimensions. On the entrance level, the beamed reception gallery ran the entire length of the entrance block and led in to the house's east and west wings. The floor was paved in Adler's distinctive checkered black-and-white marble tile, here in a harlequin pattern that accentuated the length of the gallery. The walls were of imported Jacobean oak paneling, and identical swagged reliefs of wooden fruit, locally carved, outlined the doorways into the two wings.

The west end of the reception gallery opened into the principal stair hall. Wainscoted in oak, it had three keystone-arched doorways, and a monumental carved staircase leading downstairs gave the first indication of the house's opulence. The double-height stair hall, with its towering wall of leaded glass windows, was anteroom for an impressive procession of rooms: library, music room, and dining room.

Dorothea Walker, a long-time contributing editor for *House and Garden* magazine, described Mrs. Clark's library as the warmest and most welcoming room in the house. According to Agnes Albert, the family spent a great deal of time there. Among the exceptional appointments of the room were pegged parquetry from a castle in France, and antique pine paneling. Leaded glass windows and built-in bookshelves reaching up to the library's fifteen-foot ceiling lined the room. A pair of elongated swags of fruit carved in high relief by Grinling Gibbons framed the chimney breast.

Above the mantel hung Sir Joshua Reynold's portrait of Dr. Samuel Johnson (1709–1784). Dr. Johnson, depicted without his wig, became a familiar figure to the Clark family and friends and to members of the Book Club of California, who were generously invited by Mrs. Clark to gather in her library each

Music room

Below: Music room sitting area

Opposite: Music room, portrait of Celia Tobin Clark by Giovanni Boldini

year on the anniversary of Dr. Johnson's birthday. Agnes Albert recalled that these meetings were rather informal and that her mother loved to sit in on them.

The Clark library drew depth and color from the glowing patina of fine wood English antiques with which it was furnished. At one end a sofa and pair of club chairs with shining green and brown upholstery were positioned around the fireplace. Adjacent to this grouping stood a handsome leather-topped English Georgian partner's desk, behind which rose a majestic leaded glass Palladian window framed by a pair of fluted Ionic pilasters. Helen Comstock, an authority on antiques, furniture, and traditional American decoration, included the library in her 1958 book, *One Hundred Most Beautiful Rooms in America*.

Through a set of paneled doors opposite the room's fireplace wall came the music room. Measuring twenty-seven by fifty-five feet, this was the most imposing and commodious room of House-on-Hill. Here, locally carved panels of Ingleman spruce lined the walls and imported antique parquet the floor. Ribbing outlined the wall panels and the wainscoting; exquisite fluting defined the succession of evenly spaced Corinthian pilasters that reached from the paneling to the cornice. From the intricately detailed cornice rose the high plaster ceiling with its patterns of rosettes, garlands, and musical instruments.

In the 1930s the music room became a grand salon that welcomed internationally renowned musicians, including the Budapest String Quartet, the Pro Arte, Flonzaley, and Lener quartets. Customarily, one hundred guests would gather for the concerts in the room that proved to be as acoustically perfect as it was beautiful. "It was like playing inside an instrument," Agnes Albert remembered.

The size of the music room was tempered by the strategic placement of a mixture of English and French furniture. Two conversation areas were set off by sofas with accompanying wing chairs and fauteuils around the fireplaces at each end of the room. A pair of tall Coromandel screens stood at opposite ends of the room's north wall; Oriental carpets graced the floor. A windowed wall of leaded glass with a balancing pair of projecting bays overlooked the house's south terrace and framed a panoramic view of

Dining room

Opposite, top: Dining room

*Opposite, bottom:
Celia Clark's bedroom*

the surrounding canyons and hills, allowing natural light to pour into the center of the house. A set of paneled double doors in oak opened from the music room onto the terrace.

Double doors also opened from the music room into the third principal room—the exceptionally beautiful dining room. Here panels of hand-painted eighteenth-century Chinese wallpaper, found by Adler in Venice, lined the walls. In varied hues of blue, green, pink, yellow, and brown on a buff ground, the paper depicted a delightful interplay of birds, butterflies, and flowering trees. Exquisite woodwork in sugar pine framed these panels. The woodwork included a dentil cornice at the ceiling line and a continuous Greek wave scroll on the door casings.

By day the room offered spectacular views of the surrounding canyons and, at night, a soft glow from the Waterford crystal chandelier and wall candelabra presaged the pristine night sky dotted with stars and moon just outside.

The dining table could seat thirty guests easily. As would be expected, the behind-the-scenes arrangements for dinners were impressive. Agnes Albert remembers that her mother managed House-on-Hill with a staff of twelve. The house had a large kitchen that included several pantries, a walk-in silver vault, and a wine room with a capacity of over 1,000 bottles. The double-height butler's pantry had a railed balcony lined with additional cupboards. An adjacent hallway led to the flower room and a service staircase.

Celia Clark's renown as a hostess extended beyond excellent food and memorable entertainment. One guest, the photojournalist Fred Lyon, remembered the evening that he attended her "dinner of the year." He arrived at the party in his "balding Oldsmobile convertible" with a near-empty gas tank, only to find that, at the end of the evening, his tank had been filled. Mrs. Clark's hospitality often included a tank of gasoline and a wash for her guests' cars.

The private side of House-on-Hill was no less opulent than the public rooms. The doors at either end of the reception gallery each led to a paired set of suites. To the east were bedroom suites for two of the daughters; beyond them lay the servants' bedroom wing. The family suites were spacious and consistently detailed with imported paneling and marble fireplaces. One of the bathrooms was tiled in Delft and floored in teak, while the other had pine floors and walls in opalescent Vitrolite. In the balancing wing were a bedroom suite for the son, a guest suite, and the master suite. Celia Clark "saw her house as big and impressive," remembered Dorothea Walker, and she felt she needed professional advice for its interior design. Adler had thought it best to visit England, where he and his client could collect the right pieces for a Tudor house. In the summer of 1929 Celia Clark, with her children in tow, rented a house on Hill Street in London and for that season, she and Adler scoured the country for furniture and accessories. Their excursions resulted in bounteous shipments to California. On this trip Adler introduced Celia Clark to Syrie Maugham (1879–1955), the legendary English interior decorator who had a shop in London. (Adler gave Syrie Maugham her start in the United States; he and his wife were her houseguests in Le Touquet not long before the tragic automobile accident that took Katherine's life.) One product of the meeting was Celia Clark's bedroom. According to Dorothea Walker, it was one of the first—if not *the* first—white-on-white rooms in the United States: Syrie Maugham virtually invented the style, in defiance of traditional English interior design. The beautifully proportioned bedroom was the one room decorated exclusively by Syrie Maugham. With its high ceiling and antique parquet floor, it served as a perfect backdrop for Maugham's subtly varied shades of white, including a richly sculpted carpet by British textile designer Marion Dorn (1896–1964) and textured raw silk upholstery for the room's spare arrangement of furniture. Even Celia Clark's "bird-cage bed with its tasseled tester" and bedside table were glazed in white, designer Billy Baldwin recalled.

The *pièce de résistance* and only source of color, wrote Baldwin, was the unusual "Swedish rough linen just this side of white," that literally hung from the walls. The color came from a scroll design, "crudely-stenciled" on the linen in a "brilliant grass green." Agnes Albert explained that, although the fabric spanned the entire wall surface of the room (excepting the fireplace wall), it was not attached. In order to preserve the fabric's integrity and give it a three-dimensional quality, it was mounted on stretchers installed along the walls.

Adjacent to Celia Clark's bedroom was her sitting room, paneled traditionally in Queen Anne oak. Across the hall was the art deco dressing room. Here, ivory-colored walls with panels and crowning cornice outlined in silvered lacquer cast a glowing sheen on mirrored niches.

By placing this wing to the rear of the house, Adler gave Celia Clark the retreat that she desired without achieving it at too great a remove: the main staircase was just outside of the suite's hallway, providing ready access to the house's principal rooms.

For outdoor entertaining Adler provided a cloistered loggia. Connected to the dining room through a pair of tall leaded glass doors, the loggia opened onto the south terrace. Inside the loggia had a slate floor and Carmel-stone walls; the austerity of a pair of monks' benches was softened by tubbed and potted plants.

The south terrace was an extension of the house. Oak-paneled doors opened from the library and the dining room onto the terrace, and a covered entrance projected out from the music room's double doors. Carrying through the Tudor theme of House-on-Hill, the entrance had a gabled roof and side walls of half-timbering and brick.

Carriage house and twin cottages; cottage on the left with addition by Gardner Dailey

The extraordinary beauty of the Clark property was particularly apparent from the terrace, which offered unobstructed views of the surrounding canyons and hills. The terrace also overlooked the sunken garden. A set of stone steps in front of the library wing led down to a gravel promenade that edged the walled garden and opened onto two separate flights of stone steps to the garden.

Rectangular in shape, the modest-sized garden was lined with flowers and shrubs, with a stately oak tree towering overhead. The garden's balustraded front opened to a third set of steps, leading to additional lawns and walkways. Isabella Worn, San Francisco's society florist and horticulturist, oversaw the plantings of this garden as well as the rose garden that overlooked the main forecourt, near the sunken tennis court.

Celia Clark lived in House-on-Hill until her death in 1965. During her thirty-some years of residence, she was, according to San Mateo historian Michael Svanevik, a "practitioner of an idyllic and leisurely lifestyle," in spite of the changes that were slowly encroaching on her secluded and privileged world.

In 1941 Celia Clark sold seventy-two acres to family friend Dorothy Pratt Barrett. On this property, which included House-on-Hill's carriage house and stables, Dorothy Barrett established her well-known horse breeding operation. Named "Eucalyptus Hill" after the avenue of eucalyptus trees, the property also became home for Dorothy Barrett and her family when she converted the guesthouse into her residence; San Francisco architect Gardner Dailey (1894–1967) designed an addition.

In the late 1950s, when the San Mateo school district needed to build a new high school. Mrs. Barrett agreed to sell thirty acres of her property to accommodate the construction of Aragon High School. Because the high school was a large building, the driveway to House-on-Hill had to be rerouted.

Dorothy Barrett continued to live at Eucalyptus Hill until 1961, when she sold the remainder of her property to neighbor and polo-playing aficionado L. C. Smith, who boarded his ponies and housed his collection of

horse-drawn carriages there. Smith's use of Eucalyptus Hill ended in 1965, when he developed the property into sixty-one residential lots. The buildings of the carriage house complex became three separate residences; the stables were razed.

Farther up the hill the College of San Mateo was under construction. In its development the college purchased through condemnation a portion of the property to use for parking lots—a sad loss of the cherished privacy that once guarded House-on-Hill. Agnes Albert said that these changes would have "shattered" her mother, but because she was in ill health, she was not aware of the disturbances. After Celia Clark died, Agnes Albert was intent on seeing the house and land preserved. A citizen's committee of Hillsborough and San Mateo residents proposed turning the house into a cultural center and opening the land to the public. However, because Hillsborough was exclusively residential, its city council agreed, with some reservation, to cede jurisdiction of

the Clark estate to a joint powers agreement between the county of San Mateo and the city of San Mateo. The city of San Mateo was adjacent to Hillsborough and, along with the county, would assume maintenance of the cultural center and the land. For the plan to succeed, San Mateo voters had to give their approval. It never came.

In early 1972, two couples from Phoenix, Arizona, purchased the Clark mansion and its remaining surrounding acreage for one million dollars. A San Mateo county superior court judge approved their plan to subdivide the land into thirty-eight half-acre plots but stipulated that the house could not be torn down for a period of five years. House-on-Hill survives to this day, on approximately six acres, and at the time of writing, it was for sale, with an asking price of forty-five million dollars. All along the hillsides, once pristine, houses dot the landscape, leaving only the heartiest imaginations to conjure the surroundings that once enveloped Mrs. Clark's world.

Mr. and Mrs. Kersey Coates Reed

Lake Forest, Illinois, 1929
Interiors with Frances Elkins
Standing

Entrance façade

Between 1930 and 1934, Adler received the greatest concentration of Lake Forest-Lake Bluff commissions of his career. Four of these six commissions were for Georgian houses, but one was for a French manor farmhouse for Joseph and Jean Cudahy (his second commission for them), and one for a Greek revival house for Edison and Jane Dick. During this period Adler designed an important North Shore house for Helen Shedd Reed, daughter of John G. Shedd, the president of Marshall Field and Company, and widow of Kersey Coates Reed, an attorney and director of the department store. The final product—a Pennsylvania Dutch stone farmhouse, which was sited beyond a grass forecourt with a small pool and a surrounding U-shaped gravel drive, exemplified the symmetry, balance, and elegance of Adler's work. The main elevation of the house was Georgian, connected by arms, "hyphens," to a pair of balancing wings, "flankers." The house was of shimmering mica stone, with contrasting white wooden shutters and marble accents around the windows and main entrance. Baroque dormers with a touch of the Gothic underscored a dentilled cornice—an illustration of Adler's ability at combining a melange of classical styles with elegance and taste. Ornamental spout heads monogrammed "HSR" in a raised script were Adler's adaptations from the Georgian period, like the monogram within the fanciful wrought-iron tracery crowning the forecourt and garden gates.

The gambrel-roofed hyphens that led to each wing were intimate in design and gave human scale to the extravagant spread of the house. Comparatively lower in height, these extensions ingeniously concealed its depth and were not merely interior passageways, as their unassuming appearance suggested. A paneled door with transom light was centered on each façade. The entrance into the flower room on the south side led Adler to incorporate a false doorway of duplicate design for the balancing pressing room. Maintaining a

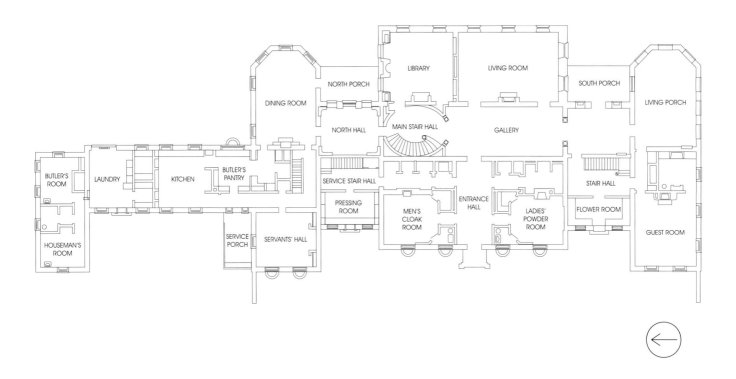

homogeneous relationship between arm and wing, the architect successfully joined the two by nestling the gambrel roof just under the cornice of the wing's hip roof. The wings, although imposing, were not as large as the main block.

A lateral extension of the service wing, which contained all the facilities necessary for the operation of the house, was segregated visually by the forecourt's gated north wall, thus preserving the visual symmetry of the main house. The service area was also framed by its own gravel courtyard.

A bluff of generous lawns and intertwining ravines overlooking Lake Michigan provided a sylvan setting for the Reed house. The curved bays of the wings projected outward toward the lake, and the rear elevation reflected the proportion and detailing established in front. On the central mass, five pairs of full-length shuttered windows welcomed nature into the house's interior. The middle pair, overseen by a marble open pediment with finial, functioned both as a doorway into the living room and the means of naturally lighting the main axis of the house. Intimate screened porches, in parallel

connection with each gambrel-roofed hyphen, also linked the house to its environs.

When the Reeds first approached Adler, it was decided that he would begin by building the tennis house that was to sit on the other side of Lake Road, across from the Reed's original house—Elsinore, an old Victorian built originally for Abram Poole, Ralph Poole's father. Helen Reed and her two children occupied the tennis house during the 1930 summer season, while the new main house was being built to replace Elsinore. Mr. Reed died suddenly in August, around the time construction was to begin. Though newly widowed, Helen Reed continued with their plans.

Classically symmetrical, the brick façade of the tennis house retained the importance of Adler's grander elevations while remaining intimate in feeling. The detailing was Georgian: a modillion course, paneled shutters, and quoins, all in wood painted white, overlooked by a series of dormer windows on the gabled slate roof. Adler's ingenious use of the site—the edge of a ravine—allowed him to reduce the apparent scale of the mammoth building by positioning the court ten feet below ground level.

Left: Garden gate

Below: Terrace façade

Overleaf: Tennis house

Below, left: Tennis house dining area

Below, right: Tennis house women's dressing room

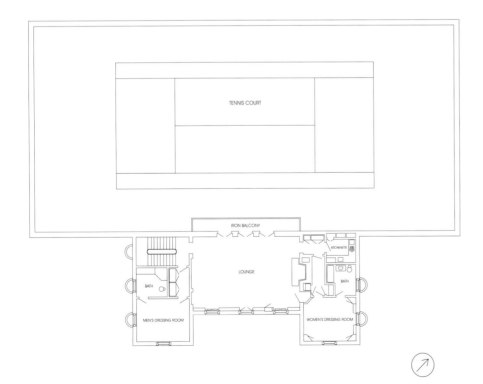

Inside, a handsome, comfortable lounge, central to the floor plan of the fore-building, was treated with the same level of attention as a principal room in Adler's main houses. The room's bleached pine paneling was detailed with fluted pilasters, cornice molding, and keystone archways. The American eagle adorned a fireplace mirror and a pair of chandeliers, introducing a federal motif. Three pairs of French doors opened onto the spectator's balcony and afforded a dramatic view of the sunken indoor court, where natural light flooded the space through a pitched glass roof. The interior ivy-covered, windowed walls created the illusion of an outdoor setting. Adler must have been delighted when, in the 1930s, tennis stars Wilmer Allison, Jadwiga Jedrzejowska, George Lott, and Frank Shields used the court for several matches during a visit to Lake Forest. The tennis court also enjoyed its share of activity from the family; Mr. and Mrs. Reed's daughter, Mary, was an avid player.

Balancing the lounge were two dressing rooms bearing the distinctive imprint of Frances Elkins's art deco style. The women's dressing room was paneled in Flexwood veneer (a flexible material of wood veneer mounted on cloth) highlighted by mirrored trim, and the floor was rubber. In the men's dressing room concentrically wood-paneled doors contrasted with plaster walls and a wooden cornice; the floor was Zenitherm, an imitation stone. Adler's eclecticism was evident indoors as well as in his exteriors.

Outside the men's dressing room, a staircase led to the tennis court below and to several bedrooms and baths upstairs. The sky-lit hallway leading to these accommodations was an arched thoroughfare, a spatial tour-de-force. Natural light from the ceiling's glass panels illuminated the hall and its succession of evenly spaced arches.

The interior of the main house, begun after the completion of the tennis house, was a major collaboration between Adler and Frances Elkins, and it was the best job of her career. Adler and Elkins were known for their excellent taste and inclination to consult with each other before making any final decisions. He was a purist who had tremendous respect for classical precedents. She, on the other hand, was extremely avant-garde. Their synergy produced splendid results. Elkins's daughter, Katherine Boyd, remarked that Adler's ability to keep her mother "in line" produced an interior truer to his style but which also contained indelible examples of her innovative design.

The decoration of the Reed house continued for some time after completion of the construction in 1931, requiring numerous visits by Elkins. Helen Reed admired Elkins's taste and, according to her son John Reed, gave her fairly "free rein." This latitude resulted in an interior of the finest and most unusual materials, which served as an extraordinary backdrop for Elkins's harmonious selection of traditional and contemporary furnishings.

The front door of the house opened into the entrance hall where a black and white marble floor glistened. A pair of Georgian marble-topped tables, with perching-eagle bases and crowning antique mirrors, foreshadowed the symmetrical order found within the house. The vestibule set the tone for the house, but was designed to suggest the proportions of a town-house, thereby intensifying the overwhelming effect of the palatial quarters beyond its handsome archway. Flanking the hall were the ladies' powder room and the gentlemen's cloakroom, both art deco in style.

The powder room glowed. Indirect lighting and yellow lacquered panels outlined in silver leaf cast a golden reflection on the room's mirrored walls and Steuben glass bolection molding (a sturdy projecting molding that was a favorite of Elkins). Uniquely patterned surfaces, including the hooded arch of the fireplace surround that projected discreetly into the interior, and deco furnishings were set off by a floor of black ebony with shiny aluminum inserts. The cloakroom was appointed austerely with

Gentlemen's cloakroom

133

*Gallery, view
toward stair hall*

*Right: Photograph of staircase
in Arthur S. Burden house
(John Russell Pope,
architect), Jericho, New York,
in Adler files*

Opposite: Staircase

furnishings by Jean-Michel Frank. Leather-upholstered club chairs, parchment-covered tables, a Giacometti bas-relief over the fireplace, and French parquetry gave this masculine interior a tactile quality.

The expansive gallery ran between the entrance hall and the living room, providing a regal passage at either end through a pair of stately black Belgium marble columns with white capitals and bases. Elaborating on John Russell Pope's design for the Arthur S. Burden house (1915) at Long Island, Adler created a sensational and imposing gallery whose shining black-and-white motif intensified the vastness of the space.

On the north end of the gallery, an elliptical hall enclosed the crowning element of the interior: a dramatic freestanding staircase of ebony and wrought glass spindles, which ascended gracefully around an English crystal

Living room

chandelier. No wonder Adler was renowned for his staircases.

The main rooms of the house, whose lay-out capitalized on the view of Lake Michigan, were all accessible from the gallery. Twin key-stone-arched doorways, one of them placed on the main axis of the house, opened into the liv-ing room. Here, an ornate mantel with accom-panying over-mantel frame served as a focal point for a room filled with fine English fur-nishings. Opposite the fireplace, a pair of antique eagle-based console tables balanced the room's center set of east windows. There was an imposing, book-lined mahogany breakfront,. overstuffed sofas and chairs upholstered in floral chintz, and Karabagh tapestry panels on the French parquet; a delicate cut-glass chandelier gave warmth to the room. The result was ele-gant and inviting.

The library, adjacent to the living room, recapitulated the monochromatic art deco theme of the gentlemen's cloakroom: tan panels of Hermès goatskin joined by coordinating stitching spanned the walls and created a cocoon-like setting. Bookcases recessed into the

Library

Library

137

North hall

Dining room

Opposite: Dining room windowed bay

walls were filled with leather- and parchment-covered volumes. A leather-covered sofa and club chair, identical in design to those in the cloakroom, coexisted successfully with English furnishings and Chinese art, all set off by Karabagh panels over French parquet. The room's finely carved fireplace mantel, doors, and casings came from an old English manor house.

The elliptical stair hall also opened to the north hall, designed as an entry to the dining room. This light-filled sitting area had a geometric ebony and steel floor, an inventive application employed earlier by Adler in the dining rooms of apartments for Laurance Armour (1928) and Harold Foreman (1928) in Chicago and subsequently in the front hall of the Long Island house he designed for Evelyn Marshall Field (1931), also with interiors by Elkins.

In the dining room, hand-painted Chinese wallpaper in turquoise, green, and brown on a golden ground adorned the walls. Taken from an English house, the wallpaper created the illusion of an exotic garden, set off by pine wainscoting and a carved modillion cornice that ended at the spacious windowed bay. A pair of pine doors with surrounding hoods led to the terrace and the north hall, and there was a pine fireplace mantel and Chinese Chippendale pagoda over-mantel—a flawless match for the English and Chinese furnishings. Embellishing upon the adjacent north hall's floor design, a deep brown wool rug with a raised geometric design was set

The Ivory Room

Flower room

on the dining room's antique French parquet. The rug was by textile designer Marion Dorn (1896–1964), one of several talented designers whose work Elkins used in many commissions.

Completing the main floor's symmetrical plan, the opposite extension of the gallery led to a second sitting area that introduced the living porch, a spacious interior used as a balance to the dining room. A vaulted gallery connected the porch to an exquisitely appointed suite overlooking the main forecourt. The Ivory Room, named for its rare ivory-posted canopy beds, provided sumptuous quarters for houseguests. Fifteen-foot walls that culminated in a cove ceiling were covered in silver foil, while old Russian silk needlepoint tapestries rested on herringbone parquetry. The tapestries, shaded in muted pastels, were so delicate that the suite had to be cleaned in bare feet. A pair of Venetian mirrors reflected the room's eclectic furnishings.

Adjacent was the flower room, both cheerful and refreshing, painted lemon-yellow. Four golden star-burst designs on a black Zenitherm floor and a graduated series of white scalloped shell

Helen Reed's bedroom

sconces, offsetting the courtyard door, adorned the interior. In the connecting hall, a staircase led upstairs to a pair of additional guest suites.

The second floor of the house provided generous quarters for the Reed family, their household staff, and visiting guests with convenience and privacy for all. A sky-lit center hall servicing the main staircase, three family bedrooms, and the boudoir was balanced by the guest and service corridors. In the main hall arched doorways opened into each room. In Helen Reed's suite exquisite parquet floors and ivory wood paneling provided a background for a selection of English and French antiques.

The original garden of the estate, lying beyond a semicircular brick wall near the tennis house, was redesigned for the new house by New York landscape architect Ferruccio Vitale (1875–1933). Vitale was well known in Lake Forest; he was instrumental in founding the Lake Forest Graduate Institute of Architecture and Landscape Architecture (1926–31), a program underwritten by prominent North Shore families, including several of Adler's clients, to advance the knowledge of design in the Midwest.

Vitale brought the Beaux-Arts principles of formality and axial planning to his redesign of the garden. He kept the built-in covered benches that ran along the brick wall, as well as the small garden pool, since this arrangement established a lovely and well-balanced "outdoor room." Centered between the benches in an arched niche stood the tall, slender sculpture of a young woman by Sylvia Shaw Judson (1897–1978).

The reconfigured rectangular garden consisted of three parallel paths running east from this area and connecting at each end to a surrounding gravel promenade. The middle path was an east-west allée of grass aligned with the main axis of the house. It was from here, through a succession of wrought-iron gates, that the main house came into full view.

Beaux-Arts design considered vistas to be an essential link between a house and its surrounding property. The integration of Lake Road into the Reed estate's orderly plan presented a significant challenge. The view from Helen Reed's garden was magnetic, drawing the viewer's gaze across Lake Road and giving the illusion of a garden path that traveled uninterrupted to the house's front door. A similar allée divided the garden north-south and ran to a gate that opened onto the driveway for the gardener's cottage, greenhouse, and garage.

Helen Reed's garden often attracted visits from garden clubs, for her famous peonies garnered a plenitude of ribbons. However, it was the newly built Adler house that turned heads during a 1933 visit. The *Bulletin of the Garden Club of America* reported that "The garden contained many fine peonies in which Mrs. Reed specializes. White tubs with white oleanders were a feature about the house. It must be confessed that the wonders of a new, very modern and extremely beautiful house by David Adler, all in exquisite taste, was a strong counter-attraction to even the most garden-minded of the Garden Club of America members."

Helen Reed later married Lake Forest widower Stanley Keith, and she resided in her house until her death in 1978. Since then the current owners, Herbert and Delores Stride, have taken enormous pride in ownership of the main house. (The Reed family retained the tennis house with its gardens and dependencies.) Their commitment to preserving one of Lake Forest's most important residential buildings and its renowned interiors is admirable. They took great pains to obtain the same yellow quilted fabric specified by Elkins decades ago for the ladies' powder room; loose wallpaper panels in the dining room were removed, relined, and reinstalled. The kitchen underwent the greatest change: it was gutted and completely renovated, but the original serving pantry, with its tiled walls and silver vault, was left intact, a reminder of the days when the woman of the house did not spend time in this wing.

Adler would be surprised to see the servants' dining hall as the comfortable and casual family room that it is today, and pleased to know that the house is still the setting of important community and family functions. Though the era of the great house has long past, the house built for the Reeds still offers a hint of the lifestyle enjoyed by its original owners. Adler was not concerned just with architecture but with creating the setting in which his clients carried out their privileged and gracious lives.

Garden, view toward house

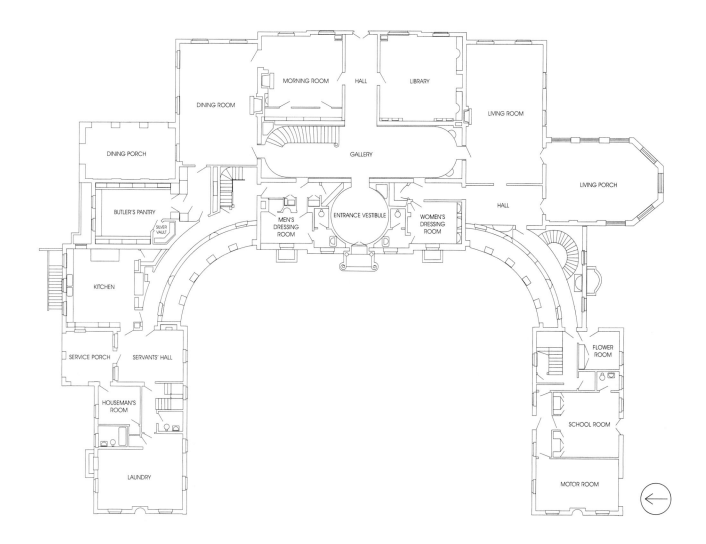

Mr. and Mrs. Lester Armour

Lake Bluff, Illinois, 1931
Interiors with Frances Elkins
Standing

David Adler's commission for the Reeds coincided with another major project: a house for Lester and Leola Armour on lakefront property north of Crab Tree Farm. Though the Armours spent their winters in Chicago, when the new house was finished, they sold their house in town as well as a summerhouse in Lake Forest on which Adler had completed some minor alterations.

Seventy-three acres of untamed wooded property that stretched from Sheridan Road to Lake Michigan provided a magnificent site for the Armours' new house, seen at the end of a half-mile-long driveway. Elm trees planted in anticipation of the new house lined the driveway like sentries, their tops meeting overhead. This cavernous allée opened onto an expansive walled forecourt, itself embraced by the whitewashed-

Opposite: House, view from allée

Left: Photograph of Hammond-Harwood House (William Buckland, architect), Annapolis, Maryland, in Adler files

Terrace façade

brick main house and its identical connecting guesthouse and service house. Behind the house, a sweeping lawn extended to the bluff's edge.

It was Mr. Armour's impression that he was to accept Adler's plans as drawn. The Armour house therefore embodies Adler's vision more purely than most of his other commissions. Adler's high regard for historical precedents is also most visible here. His plans were inspired by the center pedimented pavilion of Hammond-Harwood House (1774) by English architect and woodcarver William Buckland (1734–1774) at Annapolis, Maryland. Adler added a pair of balancing wings to his main house, producing a considerably larger building. Arcaded loggias fronted each of the wings along the curvature of the circular driveway, extending the main body of the house to its connecting dependencies. Here Adler followed the lead of his contemporary, William L. Bottomley (1883–1951), who attended the Ecole des Beaux-Arts for a short time when Adler was there, and whose talents had already contributed to the domestic architecture of Richmond, Virginia. It was Bottomley's 1927 commission for Benjamin H. Smith at Richmond that led Adler to design these curved passageways. Both architects were deeply rooted in classical design.

The Armour façade included a pediment outlined by the modillion course that also

Circular vestibule, view toward entrance driveway

Photograph of circular vestibule in James A. Burden house (Delano & Aldrich, architects), Syosset, New York, in Adler files

Opposite: View from hall through gallery to front door and allée beyond

formed the cornice. Within the pediment was an ornately carved bulls-eye window. Beveled brick quoins edged the façade and a belt course divided the first and second floors.

The Reed and Armour houses were similar in presence, scale, and siting. As at the Reed house, the rear echoed the design and detailing of the front. Full-length shuttered windows on the ground level allowed the natural light from Lake Michigan to filter into the main rooms; and the center set of windows were French doors that opened onto a vaulted hallway, giving the light a path into the center of the house.

Generously proportioned windows provided the same view of Lake Michigan from the second floor as well. Two pairs of carved stone finials balanced the projecting pediment.

At the front door Adler recessed a set of tall double-paneled doors and fanlight below an ornately carved open pediment. A pair of wrought-iron handrails anchored a delicately patterned overthrow of the same material, its apex cradling an iron and glass lantern. The doors opened onto a circular vestibule that was inspired by Delano & Aldrich's James A. Burden house (1916) at Long Island. A succession of finely detailed archways framed the vaulted hallway, bringing a view of Lake Michigan across the gallery to the front of the house.

The American eagle was a repeated theme in the vestibule; an encircling chair rail served as the ground for the plaster palm pilasters that sprouted to an outlining cornice. The uniquely shaped interior and federal detailing continued in the expansive gallery with an elliptical chamber, the whole interior unified by a checkered marble floor and a wallpaper of widely spaced, slender palm fronds that created delicate vertical pathways drawing the eye upward to the appliquéd border of Indian heads.

In the gallery twin arched niches with figurative statuary flanked double doors on the south, leading into the living room. A pair of built-in commodes served as balance to the centered archway that joined the vestibule. Another pair of doors, on alternate sides of the commodes, led to the men's and women's dressing rooms. The main staircase, also based on a Delano & Aldrich design, was placed to the right of the dining-room entrance, in the northeast corner of the gallery, and turned

Opposite: Photograph of gallery staircase in James A. Burden house, in Adler files

Far left: Gallery in Armour house

Above: Gallery staircase

Left: Photograph of gallery in James A. Burden house, in Adler files

gracefully up to the second floor. The handrail of highly polished mahogany terminated in a spiral at the base of the staircase.

The imposing gallery was planned with grand occasions in mind, but according to the Armours' son, Stanton, everyday life there was casual and their home family-oriented. He and his siblings and their two dogs were free to enjoy the entire place. On the lower level of the house Adler created three rooms, spanning the width of the house, that were devoted to fun and recreation. The largest one, the pool and card room, displayed stuffed quail and ducks mounted to its Flexwood-paneled walls. The adjacent room was for ping-pong; the third room housed a bar.

The interiors of the Armour house were a collaboration between Adler, Frances Elkins, and Leola Armour, who, unlike her husband, had a realistic sense of what the completion of a great house required. Like Mrs. Clark before her,

Leola Armour accompanied Adler to England to buy furniture. They furnished the pale celadon living room with Karabagh tapestries, Coromandel screens, and overstuffed upholstered pieces on an antique parquet floor. On the north wall a series of scrolled over-pediments crowned the fireplace and a balanced pair of doors. One of these doors opened into the gallery; the other was a false door, by now a tradition in Adler's houses, to maintain symmetry.

On the opposite wall were three tall windows, one overlooking the living porch, and providing a welcoming view of the outdoors. Adler designed an ingenious device: by sliding the bottom sash of each window toward the ceiling and releasing a latch in the underlying panel of wainscoting, the window and panel could be converted into a double door.

The living porch, with its fanlight-crowned French doors, extended the house in a southerly direction, ending in a spacious bay. To the east

*Library, view toward
morning room*

was a panorama of the lake, while to the west the doors opened onto an intimate flagstone terrace. This terrace, which also served the flower room (located in the guesthouse), linked the main house and its connecting dependency.

The Armour library, placed adjacent to the living room, on the other side of its false door, was lined with English pine paneling from a European library. Its rich patina and the deep-toned area rug made the library a warm and cozy room.

The library opened to a vaulted hallway, across which lay the morning room. Although similar in scale to the library, it was light and cheerful, with simple wainscoting and fireplace and hand-painted wallpaper in shades of aqua, blue, and green, an enchanting landscape against a cerulean blue sky. The paper, another European acquisition, was rare, and because there were not enough panels to cover the entire room, some walls were hand-painted in a

coordinating garden scene that alternated with dazzling views of Lake Michigan through the full-length windows.

The connecting dining room, used primarily for formal occasions, was large and traditionally appointed with paneled wainscoting and a modillion cornice. Above the classically detailed fireplace mantel supported by fluted pilasters was an open-pedimented over-mantel with a majestic carved eagle in its break. A portrait of George Washington hung above the mantel.

The dining room was furnished with traditional English dining chairs from Partridges, a London antique dealer, and a large, dark-brown area rug designed by Marion Dorn—very similar in design and scale to the rug in the Reed dining room. The two dining rooms were very different in feeling: the Armours' more subdued: off-white walls provided a neutral background for the luxuriant shades of brown from

Morning room

Dining room

the fine wood, richly lacquered Coromandel screens, and delicately patterned chintz curtains. An antique crystal chandelier sparkled over the dining table. Tall windows on the north wall, which converted into doors, led into the screened dining porch and to the north lawn.

The second-floor hall of the main house was, like the gallery below, elliptical in shape. Natural light filtered through a pair of skylights on both ends of this hall. On this floor were three children's bedrooms, their sleeping porch, the governess's room, and the master suite. Betty Hollins, the eldest of the Armour children, remembers choosing her large bedroom, with its views of the lake and the north lawn. She especially loved the connecting bathroom with its tiled floor, Delft-tiled bathtub recess, and wood-paneled walls, and yet another view of the lake. It was a bathroom, Betty Hollins says, unmatched by any other since!

The master suite, with its bedroom, sleeping porch, and pair of dressing rooms, provided generous quarters for Mr. and Mrs. Armour. His dressing room, which also connected to the main hall, was a handsome and masculine interior of tan marble wainscoting and flooring, with Flexwood-veneer walls. The room strongly resembled Elkins's earlier design for the women's dressing room in Helen Reed's tennis house.

Art deco in style, Leola Armour's dressing room departed completely from the traditional character of the rest of the house. The room's mirrored panels and moldings had a prismatic effect, casting a multitude of reflections. (The mirrored panels also recalled the ladies' powder room in the Reed main house.) Metal strips patterned in a delicate trellis-and-leaf design were inserted into the room's black marble floor. Indeed, these insertions were so exact that even sixty years later, the floor retained its velvety surface.

The guest and service buildings connected to the main house on the first floor. A staircase in each of these dependencies provided access to their upstairs bedrooms. By separating these quarters from the main house, Adler kept the impression of a house at a modest scale rather than a great house with auxiliary wings.

The first floor of the guesthouse contained the flower room, a single-car garage, and the schoolroom—a room unique in Adler's oeuvre. It was here that the eldest Armour children, Betty and Lester, Jr., were tutored during the summer months. Furnished as a sitting room, the schoolroom also suited the needs of houseguests. Because the guesthouse opened onto the forecourt, guests could come and go without disturbing the family.

During the late 1940s, Adler was a frequent visitor. Jean Armour recalled one visit in particular, during the late summer of 1948, when she and her husband Stanton were living at the house as newlyweds. Adler remarked to her mother-in-law, "Leola, darling, I'm doing these bungalows in California for seventy thousand dollars." To Jean, this seemed a substantial amount of money (which it was). Adler was letting his friend know how drastically his career had changed. The age of the great house was over. Commissions such as the one he referred to, for the Winslows in Pebble Beach, signified his attempt to adapt to "very different work."

The Armour house can still be viewed—as the setting for the 1978 Robert Altman film, *A Wedding*. When Altman first investigated the Armour estate as a possible location, he deemed it improbable: he was looking for a house with gardens, and the Armours' had long since gone to seed. Lester Armour's widow, his second wife, Aleka, had no intention of leasing the house to a movie company. However, after Altman saw the house, he asked Aleka Armour if she would agree to let him use it. The timing was perfect. Mrs. Armour was president of the women's board of the Rehabilitation Institute of Chicago, and one of her responsibilities was to raise money. She proposed that Altman pay a rental fee of $40,000 to the institute and hold the world premiere of the film in Chicago as a benefit. They struck a deal.

The film, about the hapless merger of a nouveau riche Southern family with an established, old-moneyed Midwestern family at a comical wedding, presents an extraordinary—and archival—view of the Armour house. Adler knew how a great house should function, and his illustrious design shines through in Altman's project.

The Armour estate, with its extensive and secluded grounds, was one of the great estates along Chicago's North Shore. Shortly after *A Wedding* was filmed, Aleka Armour sold the estate to a developer. Although the house is still privately owned, it sits on only four acres, its grounds subdivided into individual building lots, and its drive now a public road.

*Leola Armour's
mirrored dressing room*

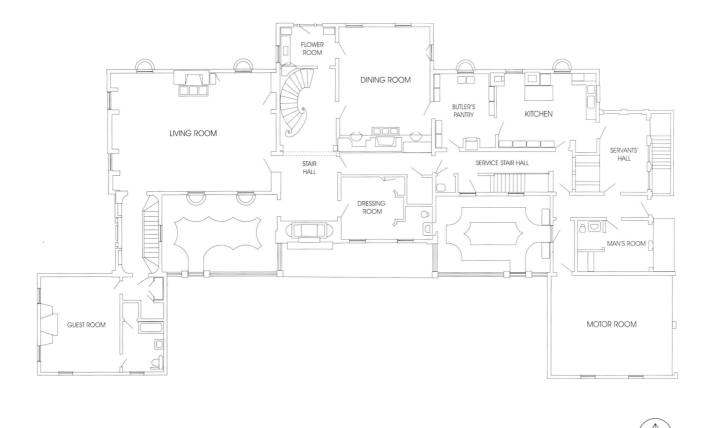

Labels within floor plan:
FLOWER ROOM
DINING ROOM
BUTLER'S PANTRY
KITCHEN
SERVANTS' HALL
LIVING ROOM
STAIR HALL
SERVICE STAIR HALL
DRESSING ROOM
MAN'S ROOM
GUEST ROOM
MOTOR ROOM

Mr. and Mrs. Edison Dick

Lake Forest, Illinois, 1932
Interiors with Frances Elkins
Standing

Adler built several of his largest houses during the early 1930s. However, the commission for Edison and Jane Dick, which followed the Armour house, produced a less imposing but magnificently classical house in the Greek-revival style. Edison and Jane Dick were newlyweds who knew Adler's work and were certain that they wanted him to design a house for them on their newly purchased five acres on Woodland Road in Lake Forest. However, they knew his reputation as well, and they worried that Adler might not be willing to work with them.

The Dick family was prominent in Lake Forest—Edison's father invented the mimeograph machine—but Adler's choice of clients was not based on status alone. He was unwilling to do anything contrary to his own taste; his clients' taste

had to be in "rapport" with his. Therefore, the Dicks were somewhat fearful when they approached Adler with a dress box full of two years' worth of clippings from *House and Garden* and several other magazines. At first they wondered if they had given him too much material; then they were afraid that their tastes might differ.

Adler, however, was enchanted by the Dicks' collection, which he found to be "remarkably consistent." From it he was able to envision easily the kind of house that they wanted. At an early meeting, he showed them a very simple red brick farmhouse, southwest of Lake Forest, near Deerfield, Illinois. Adler had been working with the Greek revival style, incorporating some elements of it into his Libertyville farmhouse and into the 1927 Clow house. He suggested the neoclassical style of the Deerfield farmhouse, and

Opposite: Entrance façade

Fretwork detail, pediment

Opposite: Side elevation, living room and guest room wing

the Dicks responded positively. He created a fully neoclassical design—and a house that was exactly what the young couple had dreamed of.

Woodland Road was a country lane with very few houses along it. Nevertheless, the Dick house would be in good company: already on the lane was a stately Howard Van Doren Shaw Georgian (1907), and across from it, Adler's house for the Reeds. Some seventy years later, the Dick house remains a landmark of the neighborhood.

From the Greek revival Adler took the house's pedimented roofline, its supporting side pilasters and half-round window, and its meandering fretwork delicately carved into the frieze. The material was horizontal flush boards painted a brilliant white, accented by dark-green window shutters. The front door was, uncharacteristically, off-center, presumably to accommodate the interior layout.

Entrance hall

Gambrel-roofed wings drawn from the Dutch colonial tradition contained a living room and a service area, balancing the main block of the house. Each gambrel roof had three pedimented dormer windows with a Greek key design in the top corners. This scheme followed closely an example from Asher Benjamin's *The Practical House Carpenter* (1832). Adler was deeply influenced by Benjamin, an early New England architect who wrote several illustrated manuals. This blending of styles was Adler's hall-mark, making each of his houses unique.

Adler's original design for the Dicks was based on his usual requirement of perfect sym-metry. Projecting from each wing was a pair of temple-like pedimented pavilions that housed, respectively, a living porch off the living room and

a garage off the service area. The porch, with its heightened ceiling, was to be the tallest space in the house; the garage was to be the same height. Adler envisioned the living porch opening onto the house's expansive property, a light-filled room that would mirror his design for two earlier hous-es (the living porch at the Clow house and the dining porch at his Libertyville farm).

However, the Dicks decided not to have the living porch. They must have been convincing in their arguments, because Adler agreed with them. Only the garage was built. Adler's original judg-ment was vindicated, however. Several years later, with children on the way, the Dicks decided to add a guest suite—which Adler designed along the dimensions of the never-realized living porch, thereby conferring perfect symmetry on the house.

Although the Dick house was on a scale more intimate than the monumental houses for which he was renowned, this commission was a masterpiece of classic beauty and refined detail. The side elevation was a triumph of Adler's eclecticism: the perfect integration of two different roof styles—shapely gambrel and tailored pitched Greek revival. The classical gable anchored the one-story guest wing, while the master bedroom suite on the second floor was set below the umbrella of the two-pitched gambrel. Jane Dick was especially partial to the gambrel roofs and remembered that Adler referred to them as "his own adaptation of a mansard roof."

The first floor of the house encircled a spacious entrance and stair hall, its space heightened by a large oval recess centered in the ceiling. Fluted casings surrounded the window and doorways, the main entrance, and the expansive archway between the entrance hall and the stair hall. The archway framed the striking circular staircase with polished black ebony handrails and stair treads. The staircase spiraled upward two floors to an oval domed skylight. A color illustration in Adler's client file—possibly one of the clippings that the Dicks had given him—inspired the unusual design for this staircase.

On opposite walls of the entrance hall hung federal-style bull's-eye mirrors above matching demilune console tables. One of these was antique; Adler commissioned William J. Quigley and Company to duplicate the original. (The Quigley firm also crafted the mirrors.) Lacquered jet black, the tables were edged in a Greek key design painted in gold. Off of the entrance hall were the dressing room and living room. In the living room, Adler and Frances Elkins created a feeling of warmth and coziness. The furnishings were primarily English; the focal point was an antique Adam mantelpiece in English pine sided by two pairs of semicircular fluted pilasters, the mantel shelf underscored by pellet molding. A carving of an oil lamp projected from its center section and a pair of rosettes decorated its top front corners.

The Dicks saw the mantel at an antique shop during a visit to New York and returned to Lake Forest with a photograph to show Adler. He approved it, but advised his clients to let it go into an upcoming auction, where it would probably go for a third of the shop's asking price. The Dicks asked Eddie's sister, Mabel Swan,

Entrance hall, detail

Overleaf, left: Circular staircase

Overleaf, right: domed skylight

Photograph of unidentified staircase in Adler files

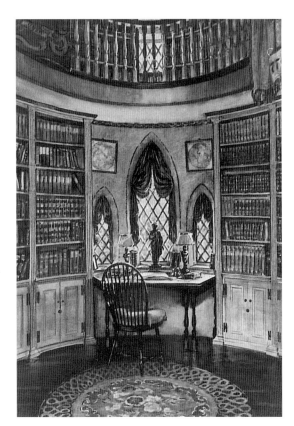

Living room, view toward fireplace and Gothic-arched bookcases

Photograph of unidentified Gothic-style arch in Adler files

Opposite: Living room, Adam mantelpiece

who lived in the New York area, to attend the auction, and set the shop's price as their limit. Mabel Swan reported that she had obtained the mantel—at a price considerably above the limit. She generously paid the difference in the price but told her brother and sister-in-law that it would be their Christmas present for the next ten years. Adler, no doubt pleased to have the mantelpiece, nevertheless must have been chagrined by his miscalculation.

The living room walls were spruce-paneled, the wainscoting herringbone-patterned. Adler took the pellet design from the mantel for the cornice molding. The rich patina of the mantel dictated the coloration of the living room woodwork. Fifty years later, Eddie Dick recounted the painstaking process that Adler used to achieve it. First, a mustard-colored stain was applied to the walls and left to settle for six weeks. Then the stain was rubbed off and the walls were covered in a whitewash, which was rubbed down with steel wool. The walls remained as created for five decades.

Adler's characteristically unusual touches in the Dick's living room included a shelving design from an apothecary shop in Charleston, South Carolina: Gothic-style arches were incorporated into the handsome woodwork, crowning the built-in bookcases.

Jane Dick recalled Adler's superb sense of proportion, especially in her living room, where she said that a party of guests could easily be accommodated but which remained cozy and welcoming to her when she sat there alone.

A one-story wing off the living room, consisting of a guestroom and bath, was added to the house in 1935. A mirrored and wood-paneled vestibule introduced this suite with its tall cove ceiling. The room featured an English-Regency style mantel and over-mantel with a crowning pediment supported by two pairs of pilasters. In the hallway adjoining the guestroom, offsetting a central doorway to the outdoors, were built-in bookcases topped with Gothic-style arches. Adler liked this apothecary shop motif, and used it throughout the house.

The Dicks needed a dining room in which they could comfortably host family dinners—they planned for children and grandchildren—and also entertain distinguished guests (Adlai Stevenson, for example, was a good friend).

The dining room windows were counterparts to the windows in the dressing room and powder room at the entrance and could not be perfectly centered in the dining room. The imbalance was artistically solved by Adler, according to Jane Dick. To achieve the illusion of balance for the two windows, he positioned an antique mahogany corner cabinet in the northeast corner to hold Jane Dick's collection of rare and beautiful porcelains.

Centered in the ceiling above the dining area was a plaster rosette that reflected in the rich patina of the mahogany table. With its leaf-patterned spokes the rosette was lovely and delicate and might have been the perfect overture for a chandelier—but Adler, Elkins, and the Dicks chose candlelight for the room, giving the room the ethereal quality of soft flickering light.

On the second floor natural light from the skylight filled the stair hall, which led to the master suite, two family bedrooms, and the sitting room. In the master suite a vaulted hallway with a succession of pointed arches led into the suite's bathroom, dressing room, and spacious,

Dining room

light, and airy bedroom with spectacular views of the surrounding ravines.

Ravines are an important aspect of Lake Forest topography, and Adler placed the Dick house to take full advantage of this natural beauty. The rear of the house featured an expansive flagstone terrace that overlooked this dramatic landscape feature.

Small, identical, hedge-lined gardens, recessed behind gated whitewashed wooden fences, edged the front of each wing of the house. The fences were another element of Asher Benjamin's influence; he had written that fences were suitable for the enclosure of a country residence.

The balance of the property was designed by Pittsburgh landscape architect Ralph E.

Griswold (1894–1981). Jane Dick was an avid gardener and, during her lifetime on Woodland Road, she graciously shared her greenhouse with the Lake Forest Garden Club.

Edison and Jane Dick were among David Adler's youngest clients, and they enjoyed their house for over sixty years, raising their children there. The house was the setting for many special occasions, including the Dicks' fortieth, fiftieth, and sixtieth anniversary celebrations. The parties for the first two of these anniversaries were grand, tented affairs with a full orchestra. In an oral family history Jane Dick recounted that one of the oldest guests at the fiftieth was William McCormick Blair, age ninety-seven. How fitting it was for him to be in attendance: he also must have thought about his friend and architect

David Adler, who had designed the Blair house in Lake Bluff fifty-four years earlier. Adler's was a career among friends, and the Dicks—who came to him so timorously with their box of clippings—became, in time, good friends.

Edison Dick died in 1994. Jane Dick lived in the house for sixty-four years; when I returned to the house in 1996, I stepped into a bygone era. She had faithfully maintained the house—even taking the extraordinary step of having the décor refreshed by Frances Elkins's daughter, Katherine Boyd. An exceptionally rare feeling of originality permeated the house; the charm, grace, and elegance of the 1930s beat still with vitality. Jane Dick was one of the last of Lake Forest's grand dames. With her death in 1997, Adler's last surviving client passed away.

Winslow dining room

PART IV

ADLER'S LAST COMMISSIONS
1935–1949

Monumentalism on the Decline

Wheeler house,
entrance façade

Lolita Armour house,
entrance façade

As the Depression tightened its grip on the country, the era of the American great house ground slowly to a halt. After the successful completion of the Dicks' house, Adler designed two Georgians—for Leslie and "Pat" Wheeler and Mrs. Lolita Armour, both in Lake Forest, in 1934. These commissions were among the last on which he collaborated with his sister. Then Adler, too, began to slow his pace, the result of his serious riding accident in 1935. Given the economy, the state of his health, and the lag in construction during World War II, it is not surprising that three of the seven commissions Adler received in the last phase of his career were never built. William and Isabelle Clow, the only clients for whom Adler designed three houses, did not build the last—a winter house designed for Palm Beach in 1937. Isabelle Clow herself was in poor health (she died in 1939). The clapboard house was U-shaped and informal: entrance was through a pair of French doors that opened from a covered porch directly into the living room. A one-story wing contained

the family bedrooms; the balancing wing had the kitchen, a bedroom, and a porch on the first floor and four maids' rooms upstairs.

The second unrealized design was a manor house in New Orleans commissioned by Edgar and Edith Stern. (Edith Stern was from a prominent Chicago family; her father was Sears Roebuck president Julius Rosenwald.) The Sterns lived in New Orleans in a colonial-style house that they had built during the early 1920s. In 1935, after acquiring additional acreage, they hired Ellen Biddle Shipman (1869–1950) to design their gardens and this in turn inspired them to ask Adler for a new house that would relate better to Shipman's design.

It is clear that Edith Stern and Adler experienced some disagreement, early on, over the plan. Though Edith Stern wanted an Adler house, she would not allow that desire to overshadow her primary intentions for the dwelling. She wrote to Adler that she "could not tell you how to build a house." But by the same token, she did not want a house that would be a "burden" to her.

Mrs. Stern called off the project. In a letter wrought with emotion, she explained to Adler that after spending an almost sleepless night "pouring over blue prints with a scale rule," she had decided not to proceed; the house was just too large and the placement of the rooms displeased her.

A third house, planned for Adler's long-standing client Pauline Palmer in 1946, for a spectacular site overlooking Sarasota Bay in Florida, would have provided a distinct contrast to the Spanish villa that Adler had designed a few miles to the south for Stanley and Sara Field in 1925. (The Fields and the Palmers were good friends from Chicago, where their families had forged a strong business relationship. Stanley's uncle Marshall had purchased Potter Palmer's flourishing retail operation, which would eventually become Marshall Field and Company.) Pauline Palmer's decision not to build was independent of Adler. She owned a house in Bar Harbor, Maine,, where a fire devastated the seaside community in 1947. Pauline Palmer abandoned her plans for Sarasota.

Adler's design for Pauline Palmer was based on the work of Mies van der Rohe, whom he deeply admired. It is an interesting sidelight to learn that Adler recommended Mies to Chicago's Armour Institute of Technology (now the Illinois Institute of Technology). As the story goes, one day in 1936, while "coming down the steps of the Art Institute," Adler encountered John Holabird and Jerold Loebel, two members of the search committee, which was seeking a suitable head for the architecture department. When they asked Adler if he was familiar with Mies, he responded enthusiastically. He insisted that the men follow him to the museum's Burnham Library, where he showed them photographs of Mies's striking Barcelona Pavilion for the 1929 International Exposition in Spain. In part, certainly, Adler's ebullience led to Mies's appointment to the Armour Institute in 1938. Mies was grateful to Adler, whom he regarded as a man of "dedication and perfectionism," and in appreciation presented him with a series of signed photographs of the Barcelona Pavilion.

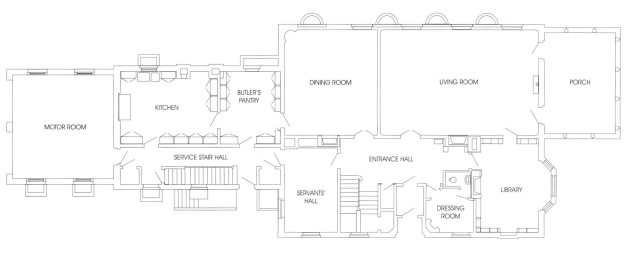

Mr. and Mrs. Louis B. Kuppenheimer, Jr.

Winnetka, Illinois, 1937
Interiors with Frances Elkins
Standing

Despite the disappointments, the end of Adler's career was not without its accomplishments. Louis and Jane Kuppenheimer were newlyweds who were overwhelmed by the enormous Howard Shaw house in which Louis had been raised. Finding the house uncomfortably sprawling, they initially sought an architect to modify it. The Kuppenheimers learned about Adler from their lawyer, who also worked for the architect. Adler told the Kuppenheimers that the only way he would work with them was if they razed the Shaw house. He knew that they wanted a more manageable house, and he was prepared to design it for them. In fact, Adler came to call the Kuppeheimer house his "bungalow," though the house was certainly not the smallest of his oeuvre.

Adler designed a smaller house, comparatively, for the Kuppenheimers, but it was brilliantly sited, facing north and atop the rise of the six-acre property. He retained Shaw's original grand entrance gate. With its massive brick piers, forged iron–grilled doors and decorative overthrow, the gate framed the new house and contributed a monumental quality commonly associated with Adler's much larger houses.

The Kuppenheimer house was a whitewashed brick building of French and Georgian derivation that was set beyond a square-walled and pebbled forecourt. The design of the house was very simple, consisting of a center block with a mansard-roofed single wing to the east for the service area and garage. In place of the usual balancing wing was a wonderful sun porch that was aligned with the back of the

Opposite: Kuppenheimer house, view through Shaw gates

house, along with a charming bay that projected toward the west from the library.

The front entrance was arched, with a concave edge that framed the recessed front door and fanlight. Inside was the vestibule, a vaulted interior with Zenitherm flooring in a herringbone pattern and a paneled wainscot that led through a second door into the house's spacious entrance hall. This led, in turn, to the principal rooms—dining room, living room, and library—and housed the main staircase.

A striking feature of the Kuppenheimer house was its copper hipped roof—as the house aged, the roof took on a rich greenish patina that glowed in the sunlight. In the extremes of Chicago's climate, severe temperature changes caused the metal to expand and contract simultaneously (or so it seemed). Many years later, Jane Kuppenheimer, whose affection for Adler neither time nor leaking roofs had dimmed, reflected that the great architect wasn't always the most practical! However, she added, he was, without doubt, exceptional when it came to detail and achieving overall perfection, like the copper downspout heads that were copied from models at the Art Institute of Chicago. Adler spent weeks obtaining special permission to have gelatin molds made of the originals. Wing-shaped, with a scalloped edge, the heads were detailed with raised ornamentation: a fleur-de-lis at the base and three rosettes at the top. The attention to detail was pure Adler. Regardless of how large or small the commission was, he always strove for excellence.

For the garden side of the house, Adler used similar elements to those of the Reed and Armour houses. Again he specified full-length French doors across the house's main block, opening onto a broad and private flagstone terrace. Overlooking the garden, the terrace provided an appealing space for relaxing and entertaining. At the west side of the house it wrapped around to meet the sun porch, where Jane Kuppenheimer could sit and enjoy the property's natural setting while basking in the radiant sunlight that poured in through the room's French doors.

Adler wanted Frances Elkins to collaborate with him, but the Kuppenheimers were hesitant to hire her because of her reputation for exceeding budget. According to Jane Kuppenheimer, Elkins assured her that if she and her husband

stuck to their decisions, she would be able to keep on budget. The Kuppenheimers agreed, but Louis Kuppenheimer suggested, tongue-in-cheek, that Elkins might decorate the entrance hall and he would put up a sign that said "Decorated by Frances Elkins"; he and his family would live upstairs.

Elkins completed the job on budget, assisted, as Jane Kuppenheimer recalled, by Elkins's secretary, Harriet Wheel. She telephoned Elkins daily in Europe, where she was buying, to review the purchases. Among them were, of

Entrance façade

course, Jean-Michel Frank ebony tables and leather chairs and handmade plaster lamps by Giacometti.

The living room was primarily art deco, its plaster walls faux-painted to resemble wood, with their rounded corners extending to the curved cove ceiling. On the mantel, bolection molding in Steuben glass sparkled from the natural light that poured in through the wall of French doors opposite the fireplace. Elkins loved Steuben glass; two pairs of carved wood

and glass sconces graced the living room. The mantel glass was enhanced by a penetrating base of silver leaf, which turned a radiant orange-gold over time.

The living room opened west through a pair of doors to the light-filled sun porch. Adler placed two pairs of paneled doors on the fireplace wall. One pair opened to the entrance hall, but the second pair, which he aligned with the library, functioned differently: a smaller, single false doorway was inconspicuously cut into the paneled design, thereby maintaining the symmetry in the living room and preserving the adjoining wall of built-in bookcases in the library.

The oak-paneled walls, built-in bookcases, and cove ceiling of the library created a cozy ambiance. A pair of tall fluted pilasters framed the travertine mantel; opposite, the projecting bay of windows, dominated by a large arched window, filtered comforting rays of natural light into this intimately scaled interior.

A small hallway connected the library with the entrance hall. Here, Adler placed a shallow niche with shelves where the Kuppenheimers could display objets d'art. The fluted pilasters of the niche echoed the detailing from the fireplace wall in the library.

In the dining room the buff-colored Zenitherm floor designed by Adler was bordered by a series of identical star designs. An arched full-length niche, edged with a border of marbleized Delft tiles, was nestled on a forty-five-degree angle in the dining room's southeast corner. The wainscoting was wood-paneled in a geometric design that also bordered each of the room's doors. Two doors offset the fireplace, one leading into the entrance hall, and the other, false; the third door led to the butler's pantry. Opposite the fireplace, a pair of French doors overlooked the garden terrace.

From the entrance hall the main staircase led upstairs to the family bedrooms and downstairs to the games room. The staircase was simple, with a stunning metal railing in Chinese Chippendale. The wainscoting on the staircase wall—as in several of Adler's houses—mirrored the pattern of the rail's mahogany capping. On the steps was a Moroccan stair runner—one of Elkins's trademarks.

Downstairs, the art deco games room had what Adler called a "black-red" rubber tile floor in a marquetry pattern bordered with a Greek wave design in contrasting shades of black-red and buff. Two narrow bands in alternating red and buff enclosed the wave design. Another set of outlining bands in black-red and a "special" red encircled the design. The dark-toned room received light from three small windows on the south wall (aligned with the French doors on the first floor). To accentuate them, Adler framed the inside of each window with a pair of full-length shutters which, along with a series of plaster shell sconces, cleverly provided light:

the sconces shot light toward the ceiling and the shutters glowed from their lining of indirect lighting. A projection booth for movie screenings was also built into the room.

The second floor of the house contained the master suite, four bedrooms with connecting bathrooms, and the servants' quarters. Frances Elkins decorated the master suite with unusual textured materials. The four doors serving the suite were paved on the bedroom side in a smooth veneer of capiz shells, a unique and beautifully opalescent material, also used on the bureau and nightstands fabricated by William J. Quigley and Company.

The master bathroom had mosaic glass tiles in buff and black; on the floor alternating wavy and straight bands of tile in the two colors created a shimmering contrast, enhanced by white marble wainscoting. Everywhere in this rather small room were potent reflections. The room's white fixtures, art deco sconces, and an encircling band of the Greek key design in buff and black mosaic that ran between the marble wainscoting and the bathroom's upper walls all combined to create an exquisitely original interior.

Adler was still able to give his clients a house that met their needs and contained the balance and proportions of his grander projects. Jane Kuppenheimer said that she and husband could not have been happier working with him. Like Edison and Jane Dick, the Kuppenheimers were young when they met Adler and learned from him. Jane Kuppenheimer said, "David had the ability as an architect to create a work of art. His balance and design [were] incredible and his artistic eye was superb in all areas. Adler's design quality lived on forever. He stuck to the pride and beauty of the best of the old architects. His taste was incredible and he was precise."

The Kuppenheimers raised their two children in their Adler house and lived there until Jane Kuppenheimer's death in 1985. Then the house was sold to a young couple with a growing family. Thus began a unique second act for an Adler house. Thomas and Josephine Linden were the perfect successors to the Kuppenheimers. They enjoyed their house. In fact, they documented it, interior and the exterior, on video: an architect shows the house room by room, with appropriate narration. It is an

View of garden

important document that preserves the house in its original surroundings—surroundings that would soon change dramatically.

In 1990 the Lindens moved east and sold the house. The new owners had special needs and, because the house could not be modified to meet these needs, they applied for a demolition permit. This action triggered the interest of historic preservationists, including the Landmark Preservation Council of Illinois (LPCI). In the face of intense opposition to demolition, the new owners agreed to give the house to anyone willing to pay for moving it. Though interest in the Adler house poured in from around the world—the final list numbered forty-five applicants—the LPCI and the new owners selected a candidate close to home: neighbors whose house across the street had been damaged by fire.

Architects, lawyers, engineers, and a variety of consultants were required to coordinate the transferral by the Dell-Mar Moving Company, which cost around $200,000. Dell-Mar's owners and operators, Dell and Jim Davis, fifth-generation structural movers, blasted eighteen evenly spaced holes, several feet in diameter, into the house's foundation. Steel beams threaded through the openings became the foundation for the house at its new location. A platform of hardwood cribbing was built under the beams; powerful hydraulic jacks on dollies eased the house sideways from its original base. Winches drew the house gradually on a path of cribbing to the new site, four hundred feet away.

View of front

Mr. and Mrs. Frederick Keith

Sarasota, Florida, 1938
Razed

Adler built three houses after the Kuppenheimer house, and though he jokingly called that his "bungalow," all three were smaller. The first, a modest one-story, was designed with the utmost affection for his brother- and sister-in-law, Frederick and Elizabeth Keith, who wanted a getaway. The Keiths had bought two-and-a-half-acres of land from John Ringling on Lido Key, overlooking Sarasota Bay. (Adler knew Sarasota. In addition to Frederick and Elizabeth Keith, Adler's in-laws, Edson and Nettie Keith, also wintered there, as did Stanley and Sara Field and Potter and Honoré Palmer—of Adler's Chicago clientele.) The house was to have only a master bedroom and a small second bedroom, as a precaution against houseguests. Adler's house, while perhaps too large to be considered a cottage, was similar to the recreational buildings that he had designed for larger estates.

Its living room opened onto a bayside terrace, which formed an ell on two sides of the house in order to service the master bedroom and the dining room. Around the living room were two bedrooms, a bathroom, dining room, and kitchen. Though the house was basic and spare, as requested by the Keiths, Adler included his usual special touches, such as the plaster conch-shell sconces on the living room walls.

According to Dr. Frederick Keith, Jr., his Uncle David spent very little time in Sarasota, but his Aunt Katherine visited her parents in their Italian renaissance villa there during the winter. When she stayed at their house, she slept in the second-floor bedroom—which today is referred to as the "David Adler bedroom." (The Edson Keith house is now the Sarasota County Phillippi Estate.)

Entrance façade

Mr. and Mrs. John P. Kellogg

Salt Spring Island, British Columbia, 1939
Standing

Adler's penultimate commission for a new house came from John and Mickey Kellogg of Libertyville who traveled each summer to escape Chicago's heat. One summer season, they visited Salt Spring Island in British Columbia, where they fell in love with a farm of several hundred acres owned by an English couple. The Kelloggs bought it and began to plan for a new house.

Adler was not the Kelloggs' first choice. Mickey Kellogg met Adler at a dinner party in Libertyville and told him she was displeased with her architect. Later, Adler looked at the first set of plans and told her that they were "all wrong." When he asked why she hadn't hired him to begin with, she replied, "You're too expensive." Nevertheless, the first plans were abandoned and Adler received the commission.

Adler designed a "dream house" for the Kelloggs. They were a family of six, and the house had to accommodate a lot of guests as well. The one-story house, planned around a central courtyard, was sided and roofed in natural cedar shake, contrasting with white six-over-six mullioned windows and their brilliant blue-green shutters. The front of the house, edged with an open-sided porch, faced the water toward Vancouver Island. The living-dining room, master bedroom, and kitchen provided wonderful views in the same direction.

The expansive living-dining room was paneled in cedar planks that reached up to a tall ceiling with hand-hewn timber beams. A pair of halls opened into covered passageways leading to the courtyard, to the servants' wing near the kitchen, and to the children's wing, located

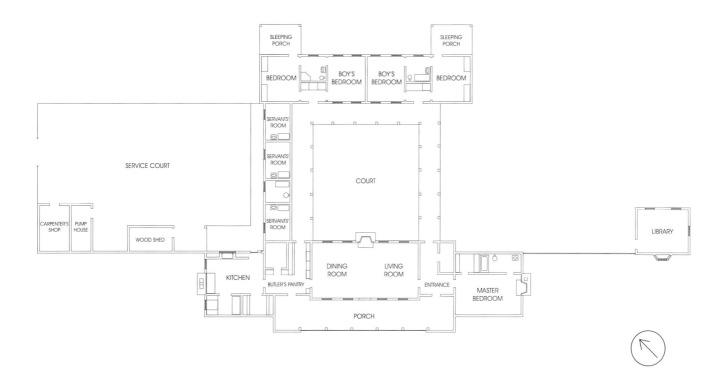

across the courtyard, completely separate from the principal core of the house. Bob Kellogg recalled the children's wing as a place where he and his siblings could "raise hell" without disturbing their parents. Two separate sleeping porches projected from the children's wing: one for the boys and one for the girls.

This was a family house—it is still in the same family—that could easily accommodate twenty for meals around the dining room table. Time spent at the house was focused on family surrounded by nature. A private study, in its own building but close to the house, offered complete peace and tranquillity.

British Columbia was distant from Chicago, and travel time to the house was substantial: it took three full days and nights on the train to get across the country. While the house

was being built, the family—along with the nurse and a handyman—stayed at the Chalet Inn in Sidney on Vancouver Island. From Sidney, they commuted daily by boat to Salt Spring Island to watch the construction. The building materials were barged in from Vancouver Island to a government wharf on the Kellogg property. From here, a Clydesdale team hauled the shipment to the site, half a mile away. The construction crew—twelve locals from Vancouver Island—also commuted daily by boat to the island.

Adler's commission for the Kelloggs was unique: Although he was no stranger to working long distance—La Pietra was built in Hawaii for Mickey Kellogg's first cousin, Louise Dillingham—Adler never saw Salt Spring Island or his completed design.

Entrance façade

Mr. and Mrs. Paul S. Winslow

Pebble Beach, California, 1948
Interiors with Frances Elkins
Standing

Adler did, however, visit the site of his next—and last—commission to be executed: a house for his close friends Paul and Ruth Winslow. Ruth Winslow headed Del Monte Properties, Samuel F. B. Morse's company, whose focus was developing Pebble Beach. When it came time to build her own house, she turned to Adler. She asked him to view the parcel of land first—which he did. The Winslow property was perched on the rise of Del Ciervo Road, just off Pebble Beach's famed Seventeen-Mile Drive, with a spectacular view of Carmel Bay and a forest of trees including Monterey pines and oaks.

The Winslow house was to be small, and although Adler clearly felt the constricting reality of downsizing, the house he designed for the Winslows still recalled the elegance of the great

house way of life. The Winslows had no children; the house was designed for the two of them. An attractive and social couple who had moved from Hawaii to help Morse develop Pebble Beach, they became members of the resort's inner circle. Their house, though simple, embodied Adler's classic design and impeccable taste.

Built low to the ground, one-storied and sided in flush boards painted white, the design consisted of a central living room balanced by two symmetrical wings—the dining room and service wing and the master bedroom wing. These wings were subtly angled to embrace the entrance forecourt, a plan that optimized the views from the house and allowed the structure to fit comfortably within its less than half-acre lot.

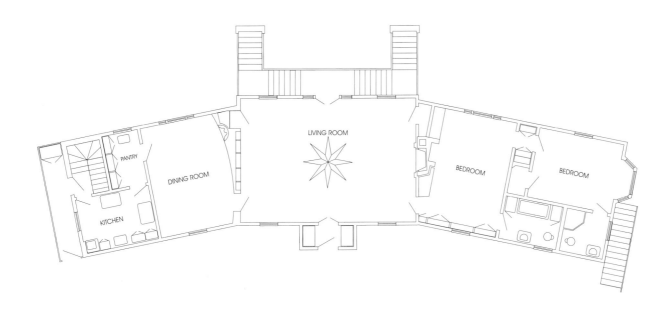

White paneled shutters gave soft definition to the three pairs of windows overlooking the forecourt, and a marquee over the front door conveyed the sense of grand entrance that Adler so valued, no matter the size of the house. Adler's original drawing for the forecourt showed a pair of entrances, but when the house was built, the plan was altered to include a single but wider one.

The forecourt met the challenges in size and topography of the Winslows' property: it doubled as a lovely outdoor room, thereby maximizing the usable area of the land. A pair of wooden benches from Adler's own Libertyville farm fronted the two wings.

Although the Winslow house was only one story high, its hillside site allowed Adler to create a lower terrace at the rear. A staircase that edged the house's bedroom wing also provided access to the terrace from the entrance forecourt. With the lower terrace Adler created another inviting outdoor space where the Winslows could enjoy the natural surroundings. It also served as a space for entertaining: a dramatic double staircase fronting the center block of the house swept down from the living room to the terrace and formed the focal point of the house's perfectly symmetrical rear elevation.

The terrace also gave Paul Winslow a place to pursue his hobby: he raised orchids, and there was a greenhouse for this purpose. Here he spent a part of each day tending to his prize-winning flowers—almost five hundred varieties of them.

The spacious living room that formed the center block of the house had a pegged, diagonally planked pine floor in with a large walnut star inlaid at its center, mirrored by a towering planked wooden ceiling. Adler, Ruth Winslow remembered, was very specific about what he wanted for her house, including the nine-inch planks for the floor. He demanded that the room's door casings be perfectly aligned. This, Ruth Winslow recalled, perplexed the workmen, who didn't understand why Adler was so particular in this detail, when he had not asked them to fill in the seams of the planked ceiling and wainscoting. But Adler knew what he wanted. The ceiling was painted a crisp white, and to accentuate its height and direct the eye upwards, he hung a portrait above the wall of built-in bookcases. French doors, opening on axis to the terrace staircase, connected this atypically scaled room—considering the modest size of the house—with the magnificent outdoor setting.

The Winslows were close to Frances Elkins, and she decorated the interiors. In the living room most of the fine English furnishings came from the Winslow house in Honolulu. However, Elkins enlivened these with Jean-Michel Frank pretzel-handled plaster lamps, a pair of chocolate-brown rugs with a bold repetitive pattern of palm leaves in shades of green and white (designed by Elkins and custom-made in Kentucky), and Peruvian linen window curtains in white with green binding.

In the dining room, which had a subtly curved wall that edged the adjacent living room and a planked ceiling, Frances Elkins created, Ruth Winslow said, one of the prettiest dining rooms of her career. The walls were covered in bright red Mexican hopsacking; a band of braided fabric in black and white outlined the dining room, seaming the room's intersecting points, including its ceiling line and the top of the baseboard. Matching curtains were made

Rear façade, double staircase

from the braid-trimmed hopsack material. Jet-black horsehair covered the seats of the English dining chairs.

English mezzotints framed in black were carefully arranged on the walls, and a Venetian crystal chandelier sparkled over the dining table. The Winslows set their table in black, white, and gold when they entertained.

The balancing wing to the dining room contained the Winslows' bedrooms and bathrooms. These modest-sized rooms were aptly called "the League of Nations" because the selected fabrics for each bedroom came from two different countries. Ruth Winslow's bedroom was furnished in a French floral design that covered the fireplace wall and most of the upholstered pieces. A contemporary rug by Marion Dorn introduced a raised texture.

Paul Winslow's room was masculine: planked wood walls, painted white, and a durable English geometric fabric for the curtains and upholstery. A windowed bay enhanced this rather small bedroom, enlarging the space and also providing a greater source of natural light.

David Adler died suddenly, as he was finishing the details for the Winslow house. In fact, as noted in the overview at the beginning of this book, the Winslows were waiting in his office to discuss their house when the news of his death came. It fell to Frances Elkins to tie up the loose ends.

Under Elkins's guidance, the Winslow terrace was finished in brick. In a letter that she wrote to Adler's head draftsman, John W. Turner, Mrs. Elkins instructed him to "brick the terrace and make a small wall around the rounded part." The terrace projected out towards the woods. She also specified that there should be a brick walkway around the house on the terrace level. Her instructions were followed precisely, and the design clearly embodied her brother's taste.

Adler's last executed commission was a small but charming and classically detailed house. It was an Adler house, to be certain, even if it is difficult to think of one of his houses as being anything but large and grand. When Adler told his close friend Leola Armour that the period of the great house was over, he was correctly reading the signs of the time. Because of altered demands, neither he—nor anyone else, for that matter—was being asked to design big estates anymore. There was no longer a call for them.

Dining room

Opposite: Living room

Santa Barbara Museum of Art

CATALOGUE RAISONNÉ

The catalogue raisonné is a chronological list of David Adler's commissions taken predominantly from his job book. Projects are listed under the date first entered; when Adler returned to a particular commission at a later date, the project is listed with the original entry. The current status of the commission, when known, is also noted. When "c." accompanies a date, the date is an approximation based on date-specific commissions executed around the same time.

1911

Dangler

Mr. David Dangler
Boys' dormitory, Allendale Farm, Lake Villa, Illinois, standing

Hoffman

Mr. and Mrs. Max Hoffman
House and dependencies, St. Joseph, Michigan, standing
Additions to house, 1914

Mr. and Mrs. Charles A. Stonehill
House and dependencies, Glencoe, Illinois, razed
Alterations to house, c.1930

1912

Mr. and Mrs. Charles G. King
Servants' lodge, Lake Forest, Illinois

Mr. and Mrs. Ralph H. Poole
Dependencies, Lake Bluff, Illinois, destroyed by fire
House, 1913, standing

1913

Mr. and Mrs. William E. Clow, Jr.
House, Lake Forest, Illinois, standing

Dewey

Mr. and Mrs. Charles S. Dewey
House, North Chicago, Illinois, standing

Mr. and Mrs. Granger Farwell
House, Libertyville, Illinois, not built

Miss Anna E. Felt
Chapel, Greenwood Cemetery, Galena, Illinois, standing

Greenwood Cemetery
Iron gates, Galena, Illinois, standing

King

Mr. and Mrs. Charles G. King
House, Chicago, Illinois, razed

Mr. and Mrs. Louis E. Laflin
Alterations to service buildings, Lake Forest, Illinois

1914

Mr. and Mrs. Eliphelet Cramer
Alterations to house, Chicago, Illinois

Cudahy

Mr. and Mrs. Joseph M. Cudahy
House, Lake Forest, Illinois, standing
Casino, 1918, razed

Mr. and Mrs. John V. Farwell
Garage, Lake Forest, Illinois, standing

1915

Mr. and Mrs. A. Watson Armour
Gate lodges, garage and additions and alterations
to lodges, Lake Forest, Illinois, standing

Armour

House, 1917, not built
Poultry house and superintendent's cottage, 1917,
standing
Tunnel for lodges, 1936, standing

Mr. and Mrs. Morris E. Berney
House and garage, Fort Worth, Texas, standing

"Lakeview houses"

Mr. Ambrose Cramer or "Lakeview houses"
House, Chicago, Illinois, standing

Mr. Henry C. Dangler or "Lakeview houses"
House, Chicago, Illinois, standing

Mrs. C. Morse Ely
Orangery, Lake Bluff, Illinois, standing

Ely

Cottages, 1916, standing
House, 1922, not built
House, 1923, standing
Orangery and cottages remodeled into houses
North wing moved nearby; remodeled into
a separate house

Mr. Robert Leatherbee
House, North Chicago, Illinois, not built

Nields

Mr. and Mrs. Benjamin Nields
House, Rye, New York, standing

Mr. Abram Poole or "Lakeview houses"
House, Chicago, Illinois, standing

Mrs. Arthur Ryerson or "Lakeview houses"
House, Chicago, Illinois, standing

1916

Crane

Mrs. Neil P. Anderson
House and garage, Fort Worth, Texas, standing

Mr. and Mrs. Richard T. Crane, Jr.
House, Jekyll Island, Georgia, standing

Jones

Mr. and Mrs. David B. Jones
House, Santa Barbara, California, razed
Service building, 1917, standing
Service building remodeled into a house

Mr. and Mrs. Charles B. Pike
House, Lake Forest, Illinois, standing

1917

Mr. and Mrs. A. Rosecrans Baldwin
House, Lake Bluff, Illinois, not built

Mr. Charles I. Dangler
Headstone, Greenwood Cemetery, Galena, Illinois,
standing

Mr. Henry C. Dangler
Headstone, Greenwood Cemetery, Galena, Illinois,
standing

Mr. and Mrs. Alfred E. Hamill
Alterations to house, Lake Forest, Illinois, standing
Alterations and additions to house, 1921, standing
Garden pavilion, garage and tower, 1928, standing
Garage and tower remodeled into a house

Mr. and Mrs. Albert D. Lasker
House and dependencies, Highland Park, Illinois,
not built

Mr. and Mrs. Albert D. Lasker
Alterations to house, Glencoe, Illinois, c.1917, razed

Mr. and Mrs. Edwin S. Rosenbaum
Alterations to house and garden plan, Glencoe,
Illinois, c.1917, razed

1702 South Michigan Avenue
Chicago, Illinois

Mr. Charles A. Stonehill
Commercial building, Chicago, Illinois, not built

1918

Adler

Mr. and Mrs. David Adler
Alterations and additions to farmhouse,
Libertyville, Illinois, standing
Garage, 1926, standing
Additions and alterations to farmhouse, 1934,
standing

Adler

Additions and alterations to farmhouse, 1941, standing

Mr. and Mrs. Medill McCormick
Alterations to house and dependencies, Byron, Illinois

1919

Mr. and Mrs. Bruce Borland
Alterations to house, Chicago, Illinois

Mr. and Mrs. Kent S. Clow
House and garage, Lake Forest, Illinois, not built

Mrs. Henry C. Dangler
House, Colorado Springs, Colorado, not built

Mrs. Frances A. Elkins
Alterations to house, Monterey, California, standing
Alterations to garden, 1944, not original

Mr. J. H. Harding
Alterations to roof, c.1919

Mr. and Mrs. DeForest Hulburd
Service buildings, Lake Forest, Illinois

Mr. and Mrs. Hugh McBirney Johnson
House, Lake Bluff, Illinois, not built

Mr. George E. Keiser
Alterations to house, Lake Forest, Illinois, c.1919

McClernon
Garage, c.1919

Major Frederic G. McLaughlin
Alterations to service building, Lake Forest, Illinois, standing
Service building remodeled into a house

Mr. Ralph Owen
c.1919

Mr. and Mrs. Joseph Medill Patterson
Alterations to house, Libertyville, Illinois, c.1919

Mr. Abram Poole
Alterations to house, New York, New York

Mr. William J. Quigley
c.1919

Shore Acres Club

Shore Acres Club
Locker houses, Lake Bluff, Illinois
Clubhouse and temporary buildings, 1923, clubhouse destroyed by fire
Clubmaker's shop, greens keeper's cottage, and alterations to clubhouse and men's locker, 1928

Mrs. Leverett Thompson
Alterations to house, Lake Forest, Illinois, standing

Wilson

Mr. Oliver T. Wilson
Garage and alterations to house, Lake Forest, Illinois
Garage remodeled into a house
House razed

1920

Mr. Harvey S. Austrian
Alterations and additions to house, Chicago, Illinois

Mr. and Mrs. Edwin Bewley
Fort Worth, Texas, c.1920

Dr. and Mrs. Egil Boeckmann
Alterations and additions to house, Dellwood,
Minnesota, standing

Mr. and Mrs. William P. Bomar
House, Fort Worth, Texas, not built

The Honorable C. Campbell
London, England, c.1920

Mr. and Mrs. Charles S. Dewey
Alterations to house, Chicago, Illinois, c.1920

Mr. and Mrs. Walter F. Dillingham
House and dependencies, Honolulu, Hawaii
House standing
Dependencies razed

Mr. and Mrs. Harold E. Foreman
Alterations and additions to house, Glencoe,
Illinois, standing

Mr. Ezra P. Prentice
Alterations to house, Greenwich, Connecticut

Mrs. Elizabeth Stone
Alterations to house, Woodstock, Vermont

1921

Mr. and Mrs. Richard T. Crane, Jr.
Garden gate, Chicago, Illinois, razed

Mr. and Mrs. Potter Palmer II
Alterations to house, Chicago, Illinois, razed
Alterations to house, 1925

Ryerson

Mr. and Mrs. Joseph T. Ryerson, Jr.
House, Chicago, Illinois, standing
Garage, 1924
Addition of rooftop study, 1930

Mr. and Mrs. Jesse L. Strauss
House and dependencies, Glencoe, Illinois, standing

1922

Mr. and Mrs. A. Rosecrans Baldwin
Alterations to house, Chicago, Illinois, standing

1400 Corporation
Chicago, Illinois, c.1922

Mr. and Mrs. Owen B. Jones
House, Lake Forest, Illinois, standing
Cottages, 1926, standing
The house consists of 2 wings. The first wing was
designed by Adler and the second wing by Work in
1925. The cottages are attributed to Adler, but
probably by Work.

Mr. and Mrs. Noble B. Judah
Apartment, Chicago, Illinois, c.1922, standing

Peabody

Mr. and Mrs. Stuyvesant Peabody
Alterations to house, Hinsdale, Illinois, c.1922,
standing

Mr. George F. Porter
Alterations to house and garage, Chicago, Illinois

Mr. George F. Porter
Houseboat, Lake Geneva, Illinois, c.1922

1923

Mr. and Mrs. Arthur G. Cable
Garden house and alterations to house, Glencoe,
Illinois, c.1923, standing
Alterations and additions to house and garden,
1928, standing

Mr. and Mrs. Honoré Palmer
Alterations to house, Sarasota, Florida, razed

Mr. Harold C. Pynchon
House, Barrington, Illinois, c.1923, not built

Mr. Roger Shepard
Alterations to house, St. Paul, Minnesota, c.1923

Smith

Mr. and Mrs. Lloyd R. Smith
House, Milwaukee, Wisconsin, standing

1924

Mr. and Mrs. A. Watson Armour
Alterations to apartment, Chicago, Illinois

Atchison, Topeka and Santa Fe Railroad
Dining car, c.1924

Mr. and Mrs. John Borden
Alterations to house, Chicago, Illinois, c.1924

Mr. and Mrs. Richard T. Crane, Jr.
House, Ipswich, Massachusetts, standing
Gate lodges, 1927, standing
Water tower, 1927, not built

Mr. and Mrs. Edwin G. Foreman, Jr.
House, Glencoe, Illinois, not built

Mr. Frank A. Hecht
Alterations to house, Barrington, Illinois, standing
Alterations to cottage, 1929
Attributed to Adler, probably by Work

Judah

Mr. and Mrs. Noble B. Judah
Coach house, Lake Forest, Illinois, standing
Remodeled into a house

Mr. and Mrs. Albert D. Lasker
Alterations to house, Chicago, Illinois, c.1924

Senator James E. MacMurray
Alterations to house, Barrington, Illinois
Attributed to Adler, probably by Work

Mr. and Mrs. Honoré Palmer
House, Sarasota, Florida, not built

Mr. Robert Schaffner
Alterations to house, Highland Park, Illinois

Mr. and Mrs. Wallace C. Winter
House and garage, Lake Forest, Illinois
House razed
Garage standing

Mr. Robert Work
c.1924

1925

Mr. and Mrs. Lester Armour
Alterations to library, Lake Forest, Illinois

Barrington Hills Country Club
Clubhouse, Barrington, Illinois, destroyed by fire
Attributed to Adler, probably by Work

Field

Mr. and Mrs. Marshall Field III
House, New York, New York, razed

Mr. and Mrs. Stanley Field
House and dependencies, Sarasota, Florida, standing

Mr. and Mrs. Charles G. King
Alterations to apartment, Chicago, Illinois

Mr. and Mrs. Albert D. Lasker
House and dependencies, Everett, Illinois
House standing
Several dependencies remodeled into houses

1926

Mr. and Mrs. William McCormick Blair
House and dependencies, Lake Bluff, Illinois, standing
Tennis house, c.1928, standing

Mandel

Mr. and Mrs. Robert Mandel
House and dependencies, Highland Park, Illinois,
standing

1927

Mr. and Mrs. William E. Clow, Jr.
House, Lake Forest, Illinois, standing

Mr. and Mrs. Joseph M. Cudahy
Alterations to apartment, Chicago, Illinois, c.1927,
razed

Dangler

Mrs. Henry C. Dangler
House, Colorado Springs, Colorado, standing

Mr. Thorne Donnelley
Alterations to house and garden, Lake Forest,
Illinois

Miss J. Fortune
Alterations to apartment, Chicago, Illinois, c.1927,
razed

Mrs. Charles B. Goodspeed
Apartment, Chicago, Illinois, standing

1928

Mr. David Adler
Alterations to office, Chicago, Illinois

Mr. and Mrs. David Adler
Alterations to apartment, Chicago, Illinois, c.1928

Mrs. Isaac D. Adler
Alterations to house, Milwaukee, Wisconsin, c.1928,
razed

Armour

Mr. and Mrs. Laurance H. Armour
Alterations and additions to house, Lake Forest,
Illinois, standing
Stables, c.1928, razed
Alterations to house, c.1929
Bath houses and swimming pool, 1937
Bath houses standing

Mr. and Mrs. Laurance H. Armour
Apartment, Chicago, Illinois, standing

Armstrong
c.1928

Bentley

Mr. and Mrs. Richard Bentley
House, Lake Forest, Illinois, standing

Mr. and Mrs. Edward Bermingham
Greenhouse and kennels, Lake Forest, Illinois

Boeckmann

Dr. and Mrs. Egil Boeckmann
House, St. Paul, Minnesota, standing

Mrs. C. Morse Ely
House, c.1928, not built

Mr. and Mrs. Harold E. Foreman
Apartment, Chicago, Illinois, standing

Mr. and Mrs. DeForest Hulburd
Alterations to house, Lake Bluff, Illinois

Mr. and Mrs. Stanley Keith
Alterations to house, Lake Forest, Illinois, c.1928, standing

Mr. and Mrs. F.W. Morf
House, Barrington, Illinois, standing
Attributed to Adler, probably by Work. Adler probably contributed to the house's interior detailing

Mr. and Mrs. Melvin E. Straus
Alterations to house, Highland Park, Illinois, razed
Coach house, 1929, standing
Coach house remodeled into a house

1929

Mrs. Celia Tobin Clark
Carriage house, cottages, and stables, Hillsborough, California
House, 1930, standing
Stables razed
Carriage house and cottages remodeled into houses

Cudahy

Mr. and Mrs. Joseph M. Cudahy
Dependencies, 1929, Lake Forest, Illinois, standing
House, 1930, standing

Mr. and Mrs. Cyrus McCormick
Alterations and additions to house, Chicago, Illinois

Mill Creek Hunt Club

Mill Creek Hunt Club
Clubhouse, kennels, and stables, Lake Villa, Illinois, standing

Mr. and Mrs. Potter Palmer II
Triplex apartment, Chicago, Illinois
Floors 12 and 13 standing
Floor 11 remodeled; original detailing in library

Mr. William J. Quigley
Façade and storefront, Chicago, Illinois

Mr. and Mrs. Kersey Coates Reed
Tennis house, Lake Forest, Illinois, c.1929, standing
House, 1931, standing
Alterations to garage and potting house, 1931, standing

Mr. and Mrs. Sidney S. Whelan
House, Old Westbury, New York, not built

1930

Mr. David Adler
Alterations to house, Chicago, Illinois

Mrs. Katherine Keith Adler
Memorial obelisk, Libertyville, Illinois, standing at Graceland Cemetery, Chicago, Illinois

Mr. and Mrs. Wolcott Blair
Alterations to house, Chicago, Illinois

Mrs. C. Morse Ely
Apartment, Chicago, Illinois, remodeled

Reverend and Mrs. C. Pardee Erdman
House, Pasadena, California, not built

Mr. and Mrs. Leonard Florsheim

House, Highland Park, Illinois, not built

Foreman National Bank
Director's room, Chicago, Illinois, c.1930, dismantled

1931

Adler

Mrs. Isaac David Adler
Alterations to house, Libertyville, Illinois, standing

Mr. Isaac David Adler
Headstone, Forest Home Cemetery, Milwaukee, Wisconsin, standing

Mr. Murray Adler
Headstone, Forest Home Cemetery, Milwaukee, Wisconsin, standing

Mr. Robert Allerton
Alterations to loggia, Monticello, Illinois

Mr. and Mrs. Lester Armour
House, Lake Bluff, Illinois, standing

Field

Mrs. Evelyn Marshall Field
House and dependencies, Muttontown, New York

House razed
Dependencies standing

Mrs. Syrie Maugham
Glass over-mantel, Palm Beach, Florida, razed
For Mrs. Harrison Williams

Mr. and Mrs. Potter Palmer III
Apartment library, Chicago, Illinois, standing

1932

Mr. and Mrs. Edison Dick
House, Lake Forest, Illinois, standing
Potting house, 1933, standing
Guest wing addition, 1935, standing

Mrs. Charles Netcher
Alterations to house, Chicago, Illinois

A. O. Smith and Company
Prefabricated houses, Milwaukee, Wisconsin

1933

The Attic Club
Club interior, Chicago, Illinois, dismantled

Dr. and Mrs. Paul B. Magnuson
House, Dundee, Illinois, not built

1934

Armour gate house

Mrs. J. Ogden Armour
House, Lake Forest, Illinois, standing
Gate houses, 1935, standing
Gate houses remodeled into houses

Mrs. Amory Perkins
House, Middleburg, Virginia, not built

Mr. and Mrs. Leslie Wheeler
House and garage, Lake Forest, Illinois, standing
Garden house and root cellar, 1945, standing

1935

Mrs. Evelyn Marshall Field
Apartment, New York, New York

Mr. and Mrs. Roger C. Hyatt
Alterations and additions to house, Milburn, Illinois

Miss Gwethalyn Jones
Alterations to house, swimming pool, and bath house, Lake Forest, Illinois, standing

Mr. Honoré Palmer
Alterations to apartment, New York, New York

Mrs. Douglas Van Dyke
Alterations to house, Milwaukee, Wisconsin

Mr. and Mrs. Samuel J. Walker
Alterations and additions to house, Lake Forest, Illinois, standing

1936

Mr. and Mrs. John P. Bent
Alterations to house, Lake Forest, Illinois

Mr. and Mrs. Noble B. Judah
Apartment, Chicago, Illinois, c.1936

Mr. and Mrs. Joseph T. Ryerson, Jr.
Alterations to library, Santa Barbara, California, standing

1937

Mr. and Mrs. William E. Clow, Jr.
House, Palm Beach, Florida, not built

Mrs. Albert B. Dick
Alterations to house, Lake Forest, Illinois, c.1937

Mr. and Mrs. Louis B. Kuppenheimer, Jr.
House, Winnetka, Illinois, standing
House moved across the street from original site.

Mr. and Mrs. John P. Welling
Alterations to house, Chicago, Illinois

1938

Mr. Frederick Keith
House, Sarasota, Florida, razed

Mr. and Mrs. Edgar B. Stern
House, New Orleans, Louisiana, c.1938, not built

1939

Mrs. Theresa H. Adler
Headstone, Forest Home Cemetery, Milwaukee, Wisconsin, standing

Mr. and Mrs. John P. Kellogg
House, Salt Spring Island, British Columbia, standing

1940

Santa Barbara Museum of Art

Santa Barbara Museum of Art
Alterations, Santa Barbara, California, standing

1944

Mr. David Adler
Alterations and additions to Hacienda del Chorrillo, Taxco, New Mexico, not completed

Chicago Historical Society
Charles B. Pike Room, Chicago, Illinois, destroyed by fire

Furness

Mr. and Mrs. Thomas Furness
Alterations and additions to house and garden, Middleburg, Virginia, standing

Mr. and Mrs. Harry C. Hunt
House, Big Sur, California, c.1944, not built

1945

Mr. and Mrs. Kent S. Clow
Alterations to living room and library, Lake Forest,
Illinois

Mr. and Mrs. Alfred E. Hamill
Alterations and additions to house, Lake County,
Illinois, standing

Mr. John M. Simpson
Alterations to house, Lake Bluff, Illinois

Mr. and Mrs. James D. Zellerbach
Alterations to study, San Francisco, California,
standing

1946

Mr. and Mrs. A. Watson Armour
Alterations to apartment, Chicago, Illinois

Mrs. Austin Niblack
Alterations to house, West Lake Forest, Illinois

Mrs. Potter Palmer II
House, Sarasota, Florida, not built

Mr. J. Clendenin Ryan
Alterations to house, New York, New York

1947

Mr. David Adler
House, Monterey County, California, not built
Gardener's cottage, 1948, standing

Mrs. John Alden Carpenter
Alterations to apartment, Chicago, Illinois

Mr. and Mrs. John Andrews King
Garden terrace, Lake Forest, Illinois
Saint Chrysostom's Church

Richard T. Crane, Jr.
Altar, Chicago, Illinois, standing

1948

Mr. and Mrs. Paul S. Winslow
House, Pebble Beach, California, standing

1949

Mr. David Adler
House, Libertyville, Illinois, c.1949, not built

Mr. and Mrs. David Adler
Headstone, Graceland Cemetery, Chicago, Illinois,
standing
Attributed to Adler's principal draftsman, John W.
Turner

Mrs. Clive Runnells
Alterations and additions to house, Lake Forest,
Illinois, not executed excepting library mantel and
bookcases

Mr. Edward B. Smith
Alterations to house, Lake Forest, Illinois

**The following entries are listed
in the job book without dates
or contextual information.**

Armsby

Mr. and Mrs. Edward T. Blair
House heating plans, Chicago, Illinois

Mr. A. A. Carpenter
Alterations to apartment, Chicago, Illinois

Mr. A. A. Carpenter, Jr.
Alterations to apartment, Chicago, Illinois

Gizyka Mine
Mr. Byron S. Harvey
Alterations and additions to house, Lake Forest,
Illinois

Mr. Byron S. Harvey
Dining car

Mrs. Bernard Hoffmann
Stockbridge, Massachusetts

E. W. Hooker
Sketches, New York

Mr. Edson Keith

Mr. Charles Lipofsky
Store, Barrington, Illinois

N. M. Markwell
Sleeping porch

N. M. Markwell
Console

Mr. and Mrs. Cyrus McCormick
Alterations to house, Chicago, Illinois

Mr. Chauncey McCormick

Mr. Gordon McCormick

Mr. A. C. McCord
Alterations to house and playhouse, Lake Forest, Illinois

Mrs. Arthur Meeker

E. E. Metcalf

Mr. George F. Porter
Sketches, Chicago, Illinois

Mr. Donald M. Ryerson

Mr. Edward L. Ryerson

Mrs. William Salisbury
Alterations to apartment, Chicago, Illinois

Mr. Byron L. Smith
House, Chicago, Illinois

Sprague

L. M. Stein

Mr. Lawrence Stern
Glencoe, Illinois

Mr. Louis Stoddard
Greenvale, New York

Swift
Dining room

Mrs. D. Thompson
Mantel

Tuttle
Lake Forest, Illinois

University of Chicago
Art building, preliminary study, Chicago, Illinois

NOTES

Overview

13 **being denied entrance**: Interview with Richard Chafee, December 9, 1997.

13 **Adler's paternal grandfather**: Interview with Carol A. Zsolnay, September 26, 1999.

13 **The Adler family's clothing business**: Interview with C.A. Zsolnay, September 16, 1999.

13 **Adler's scholastic record**: David Adler's Lawrenceville School transcripts and a letter of recommendation from the East Side High School, Courtesy of The Lawrenceville School, The Bunn Library.

13 **It was at Princeton**: David Adler's Princeton University transcripts, Registrar's Records, Princeton University Archives, Seeley G. Mudd Manuscript Library, Princeton University Library. Published with permission of the Princeton University Library.

14 **By the Winter**: Letter from Bachmann at the Polytechnikum, September 13, 1996.

14 **The curriculum at the Ecole**: Interview with R. Chafee, July 5, 2000.

15 **Though Adler was the designer**: Interview with Barbara P. White, November 7, 1997.

16 **as presaged . . . he failed**: David Adler's Application for Examination for License, April 2, 1917, The Illinois State Archives.

16 **"really more a kind of employee"**: Paul Schweikher in *Paul Schweikher Oral History* (Chicago: The Art Institute of Chicago, 1984), 27.

16 **"as soon as Adler was equipped"**: *Paul Schweikher*, 25.

16 **"I am familiar with"**: Letter from Harrie T. Lindeberg to the council of The Illinois Architectural Commission, The Illinois State Archives.

16 **"as to his competency"**: Letter from Marshall Field III to the council of The Illinois Architectural Commission, The Illinois State Archives.

17 **but was so distraught**: Letter from Tony Duquette, November 15, 1998.

17 **was "a purist"**: Interview with Katherine E. Boyd, January 22, 1999.

17 **"One must go"**: Interview with K.E. Boyd, January 22, 1999.

17 **"something off"**: Interview with K.E. Boyd, January 22, 1999.

17 **"where could I make"**: Interview with Laurance H. Armour, Jr., April 4, 1996.

17 **In anticipation of**: Interview with Phoebe Bentley, April 25, 1977.

18 **It was at the suggestion**: *Santa Barbara News-Press*, January 10, 1965, D-12.

19 **"very different work"**: Letter from David Adler to Thomas Harlan Ellett, October 1, 1945, Printed with the permission of the American Academy of Arts and Letters, New York City.

19 **by his intolerance**: Interview with K.E. Boyd, January 22, 1999.

19 **which were sitting on his desk**: *The Chicago Sun Times*, October 2, 1949, 3X.

20 **"talked to David Adler today"**: Interview with Mary R. Brown, February 13, 1998.

20 **The Winslows were waiting**: *The Chicago Sun Times*, October 2, 1949, 3X.

20 **Frances's loving attention:** The details of Adler's memorial service came from a written description by Margaret Day Blake.

20 **In addition to the contributions**: *The Chicago Tribune*, November 2, 1949, III-11.

21 **he and Blair contributed**: Interview with John Gregg Allerton, August 16, 1983.

21 **"kept few records"**: Interview with William McCormick Blair, May 15, 1977.

21 **Blair also enlisted**: Interview with David S. Boyd, January 19, 1996.

Part I: The Adler-Dangler Years

24 **Stonehill had paid for**: Interview with John Wyle, December 19, 1995.

24 **the finest country house**: Anthony Hunt, "Landscape Architecture in and about Chicago," *Architectural Record*, XXXII: 166 (July 1912), 55.

28 **helped the partnership**: Interview with Roger Baldwin, February 27, 1996.

28 **"charm and spontaneity"**: "Domestic Architecture of Henry Corwith Danger, Architect: Houses Designed By David Adler and Henry Dangler," *Architectural Forum*, XXXVI: 4 (April 1922), 139.

28 **furnish the interior**: Letter from Nancy P. Rich, September 8, 1981.

29 **Chateau de Montgiron**: Richard Pratt, *David Adler* (New York: M.Evans and Company, Inc., 1970) 10. Although Pratt notes that the chateau is in Normandy, it is actually in the Loire Valley.

30 **"painted yellow"**: "Domestic Architecture of Henry Corwith Danger, Architect: Houses Designed By David Adler and Henry Dangler," *Architectural Forum*, XXXVI: 4 (April 1922), 142.

33 **"good with the grand rooms"**: Interview with B.P. White, December 13, 1995.

33 **because a man had planned**: Interview with B.P. White, February 18, 1998.

33 **never materialized**: Interview with R. Baldwin, February 27, 1996.

33 **the field contributed**: Interviews with B.P. White and Richard Poole, December 13, 1995.

33 **"a more scholarly"**: "Domestic Architecture of Henry Corwith Danger, Architect: Houses Designed By David Adler and Henry Dangler," *Architectural Forum*, XXXVI: 4 (April 1922), 137.

34 **It started with**: Memo from Reilly Nail, May 10, 2000.

35 **"arbiter of taste"**: Memo from R. Nail, May 10, 2000.

Part II: Adler's Eclectic Classicism

44 **as well as the de Medici**: Grace Tower Warren, "Island Hostess: An Italian Villa in Hawaii," *Paradise of the Pacific*, VXIII: 5 (May 1951), 39.

44 **he did not visit**: Interview with Ben Dillingham, January 19, 1996.

45 **had to lay roads**: Letter from Walter F. Dillingham to Wellington Henderson, October 14, 1929, Property of the Bishop Museum.

45 **"Entrance to the property"**: Memoranda from Walter F. Dillingham to David Adler: *Memoranda in regard to proposed new home on slopes of Diamond Head*, 1920, Property of the Bishop Museum.

46 **Walter did not know**: Interview with B. Dilingham, January 19, 1996.

47 **Originally, Japanese moss**: Interview with Elizabeth D. Wick, February 8, 1996.

50 **hedges were replaced**: Interview with B. Dillingham, January 19, 1996.

50 **it took a decade**: Interview with B. Dillingham, January 19, 1996.

50 **"keep up and take up"**: Letter from Walter F. Dillingham to A.J. Van Couver, November 16, 1922, Property of the Bishop Museum.

50 **"open and informal"**: Interview with Gaylord Dillingham, January 22, 1998.

50 **"lost her zest"**: Interview with B. Dillingham, January 19, 1996.

50 **an historic monument**: Interview with B. Dillingham, January 19, 1996.

52 **and close friends**: Interview with Ernest Hamill, April 18, 1996.

52 **"continuous"**: Interviews with Corwith Hamill, March 3, 1996 and E. Hamill, April 18, 1996.

52 **grander look**: Interview with E. Hamill, April 18, 1996.

53 **an optical illusion**: Interview with E. Hamill, April 18, 1996.

54 **"very expensive"**: Interview with E. Hamill, April 18, 1996.

54 **"cost more money"**: Interview with E. Hamill, April 18, 1996.

55 **Hamill's study . . . was austere**: Interview with E. Hamill, April 18, 1996.

58 **prize-winning dahlias**: Memo from Barbara Herst, December 12, 1999.

64 **too drafty and cold**: Carroll L. Cabot, *The Great House*, (Massachusetts: The Trustees of Reservations, 1992), 13.

64 **give it ten**: Ibid., 13.

65 **The sole mural**: Interview with Abram Poole, April 18, 1996.

67 **According to a letter**: Letter from Edwards and Sons to David Adler, March 22, 1927, Courtesy of David S. Boyd.

69 **in the basement**: Interview with J.G. Allerton, August 16, 1983.

70 **"make America want'**: *The Valve World*, I, July 1905, as cited in *The Great House*, 20.

71 **one thousand acres**: *The Great House*, 29.

71 **"who also carried out the detail"**: Leslie A. Hyam and F. Lewis Hinckley, *Important English Furniture Other Valuable Art Property From the Estate of the Late Florence H. Crane*, (New York: Parke-Bernet Galleries, Inc., 1950), Foreword.

76 **"An American Chantilly"**: Alice Woodard Fordyce, "An American Chantilly," *Country Life*, LXXX: 5, (September 1941), 30.

80 **"most comfortable room"**: Cyrill Tregillus, Reminiscences, 1971, 96.

82 **brushed the dew**: John Gunther, *Taken At The Flood: The Story of Albert D. Lasker* (New York: Harper and Brothers, 1960), 176.

82 **made various changes**: C. Tregillus, *Reminiscences*, 1971, 116.

83 **the pet project**: C. Tregillus, *Reminiscences*, 1971, 103.

83 **bodyguards in the era**: C. Tregillus, *Reminiscences*, 1971, 110.

86 **seventy-five thousand dollars**: C. Tregillus, *Reminiscences*, 1971, 94.

86 **a nearby market**: C. Tregillus, *Reminiscences*, 1971, 105.

87 **"immensely"**: Letter from Mary Woodard Lasker, April 25, 1979.

87 **"the best domestic architect"**: Letter from M.W. Lasker, April 25, 1979.

87 **loved the house before**: Interview with Robin Cerney, March 11, 1996.

88 **To shape and clarify**: Interview with William McCormick Blair, May 15, 1977.

88 **Blair and his son**: Letter from Edward McCormick Blair, December 1, 1995.

91 **the original sketch**: Inscription by Henry O. Milliken on verso of Adler's sketch, 1937, Cooper-Hewitt, National Design Museum, Smithsonian Institution.

91 **Mrs. Blair was a talented**: Interview with Dorothy Mosiman, December 4, 1995.

99 **Jane Weeden felt**: Interview with Jane Weeden, March 3, 1996.

99 **he was inspired**: Adler's files "Scandinavian No. 14," Exterior (14A) contain photographs of the Villa Primavesi, Courtesy of David S. Boyd.

102 **had been displayed**: Sargent Collier, "A Neo-Doric House Near Chicago," *Town and Country*, LXXXIX: 4137 (October 1, 1934), 35.

102 **"walls were covered"**: Interview with Mitchell Owens, November 1, 2000.

Part III: Adler Expands

111 **Initially, Celia Clark**: Interview with Agnes C. Albert, May 4, 1997.

111 **As early as**: *The San Mateo Times* (Weekend), October 29, 1966, 6A.

113 **on an island**: Interview with A.C. Albert, January 20, 1998.

114 **described Celia Clark's library**: Interview with Dorothea Walker, November 19, 1998.

114 **the family spent**: Interview with A.C. Albert, May 4, 1997.

116 **that these meetings**: Interview with A.C. Albert, May 6, 1997.

116 **an authority on**: Helen Comstock, *100 Most Beautiful Rooms In America* (New York: The Viking Press, 1958), 72-73.

116 **"It was like playing"**: Interview with A.C. Albert, May 4, 1997.

118 **Agnes Albert remembers**: Interview with A.C. Albert, May 4, 1997.

118 **remembered the evening**: Interview with Fred Lyon, January 18, 1999.

118 **"balding Oldsmobile convertible"**: Interview with Fred Lyon, January 18, 1999.

119 **"saw her house"**: Interview with D. Walker, January 22, 1998.

119 **her start in**: "An old team, a new trend: Black plus white plus color," *House and Garden*, C: 4 (April 1951), 95.

119 **be her houseguests**: Letter from Countess Camilla Chandon de Briailles, October 25, 1998.

119 **one of the first**: Interview with D. Walker, October 14, 1998.

119 **"bird-cage bed"**: Billy Baldwin, *Billy Baldwin Remembers* (New York: Harcourt Brace Jovanovich, 1974), 178.

119 **"crudely stenciled"**: Ibid, 177.

119 **"brilliant grass green"**: Ibid, 178.

119 **a three-dimensional**: Interview with A.C. Albert, May 4, 1997.

120 **"practitioner of an idyllic"**: *The San Mateo Times*, May 30, 1986, B3.

121 **"shattered"**: Interview with A.C. Albert, January 20, 1998.

121 **a cultural center**: Interview with A.C. Albert, May 6, 1997.

129 **"in line"**: Interview with K.E. Boyd, January 19, 1996.

129 **"free rein"**: Letter from John S. Reed, July 16, 1996.

134 **Pope's design**: Adler's files "Early American No. 1," Exteriors (1A) and "Modern American No. 2," Exteriors (2A) contain photographs of the Arthur S. Burden house, Courtesy of David S. Boyd.

144 **"The garden contained"**: *Bulletin of The Garden Club of America*, No. 4: Fifth Series (July 1933) 34-35, The Garden Club of America.

148 **Mr. Armour's impression**: Interview with Aleka G. Armour, March 7, 1979.

148 **Hammond-Harwood House**: Adler's files "Early American No. 1," Exteriors (1A) contain photographs of the Hammond-Harwood House, Courtesy of David S. Boyd.

148 **It was Bottomley's**: Adler's files "Modern American No. 2," Exteriors (2A) contain photographs of the Benjamin H. Smith house, Courtesy of David S. Boyd.

150 **that was inspired**: Adler's files "Early American No. 1," Exteriors (1A), and Interior Stairs (1G) contain photographs of the James A. Burden house, Courtesy of David S. Boyd.

154 **everyday life there**: Interview with T. Stanton Armour, June 14, 1997.

154 **a collaboration between**: Interview with Elizabeth A. Hollins, September 17, 1997.

155 **the dining chairs**: Interview with E.A. Hollins, September 17, 1997.

158 **choosing her large bedroom**: Interview with E.A. Hollins, September 17, 1997.

158 **"Leola, darling"**: Interview with Jean R. Armour, June 5, 1996.

158 **"very different work"**: Letter from David Adler to Thomas Harlan Ellett, October 1, 1945, Printed with the permission of the American Academy of Arts and Letters, New York City.

158 **he was looking**: Interview with A.G. Armour, March 7, 1979.

158 **had no intention**: Interview with A.G. Armour, March 7, 1979.

158 **she proposed that**: Interview with A.G. Armour, March 7, 1979.

161 **be in "rapport"**: Taped interview with Jane and Edison Dick, September 30, 1981, Lake Forest Library/ Community Cornerstones.

161 **were somewhat fearful**: Sally and Edison Dick, *Recollections of Jane Warner Dick*, (Washington, D.C.: Heritage Associates, 1993), 52.

161 **"remarkably consistent"**: Taped interview with Jane and Edison Dick, September 30, 1981, Lake Forest Library/ Community Cornerstones.

164 **an example from**: Asher Benjamin, *The Practical House Carpenter* (New York: The Architectural Book Publishing Company, 1917, Reprint of original, 1832) 125; as cited in Richard Pratt, *David Adler* (New York: M.Evans and Company, Inc., 1970) 172.

165 **"his own adaptation"**: Interview with J.W. Dick, March 16, 1977.

165 **Adler commissioned**: Interview with J.W. Dick, March 16, 1977.

168 **She generously paid**: Interview with J.W. Dick, March 16, 1977.

168 **Eddie Dick recounted**: Taped interview with Jane and Edison Dick, September 30, 1981, Lake Forest Library/ Community Cornerstones.

170 **welcoming to her**: Taped interview with Jane and Edison Dick, September 30, 1981, Lake Forest Library/ Community Cornerstones.

170 **according to Jane Dick**: Interview with J.W. Dick, March 16, 1977.

170 **fences were suitable**: Asher Benjamin, *The Practical House Carpente*r (New York: The Architectural Book Publishing Company, 1917, Reprint of original, 1832) 68.

171 **an oral family history**: Sally and Edison Dick, *Recollections of Jane Warner Dick*, (Washington, D.C.: Heritage Associates, 1993), 83-84.

Part IV: Adler's Last Commissions

174 **"could not tell you"**: Letter from Edith R. Stern to David Adler, c.1938, Collection of Longue Vue House and Gardens, New Orleans, Louisiana.

174 **"burden" to her**: Letter from Edith R. Stern to David Adler, c.1938, Collection of Longue Vue House and Gardens, New Orleans, Louisiana.

175 **"pouring over blueprints"**: Letter from Edith R. Stern to David Adler, c.1938, Collection of Longue Vue House and Gardens, New Orleans, Louisiana.

175 **a strong business relationship**: Janet Snyder Matthews, "The Fields and their Great House," *Field Club 1957-1982* (1982) 9.

175 **where a fire**: *The Chicago Sun Times*, October 2, 1949, 3X.

175 **"coming down the steps"**: Elaine S. Hochman, *Architects of Fortune: Mies Van Der Rohe and the Third Reich* (New York: Fromm International Publishing Corporation, 1990), 254-255.

175 **"dedication and perfectionism"**: Letter from Richard Pratt to Mr. Pettengill, August 17, 1966, American Institute of Architects Archives.

177 **overwhelmed by**: Interview with Jane B. Kuppenheimer, April 29, 1977.

178 **the most practical!**: Interview with J.B. Kuppenheimer, April 29, 1977.

178 **that were copied**: Interview with J.B. Kuppenheimer, April 29, 1977.

178 **while basking in**: Interview with J.B. Kuppenheimer, April 29, 1977.

178 **"Decorated by Frances Elkins"**: Interview with J.B. Kuppenheimer, April 30, 1979.

178 **review the purchases**: Interview with J.B. Kuppenheimer, April 30, 1979.

180 **"had the ability"**: Interview with J.B. Kuppenheimer, May 5, 1977.

183 **as a precaution**: Interview with Frederick Keith, Jr., July 16, 1998.

183 **Uncle David spent**: Interview with F. Keith, Jr., July 16, 1998.

184 **"all wrong"**: Interview with Phoebe Andrew, October 25, 1996.

184 **"You're too expensive"**: Interview with P. Andrew, October 25, 1996.

184 **a "dream house"**: Interview with Bob Kellogg, October 13, 1997.

185 **"raise hell"**: Interview with B. Kellogg, October 13, 1997.

185 **and travel time**: Interview with B. Kellogg, October 13, 1997.

186 **the constricting reality**: Interview with J.R. Armour, June 5, 1996.

187 **wooden benches**: Interview with Ruth Winslow, August 18, 1980.

188 **was very specific**: Interview with R. Winslow, January 24, 1980.

188 **perplexed the workmen**: Interview with R. Winslow, August 18, 1980.

188 **prettiest dining rooms**: Interview with R. Winslow, January 24, 1980.

191 **"the League of Nations"**: Interview with R. Winslow, January 24, 1980.

191 **the Winslows were waiting**: *The Chicago Sun Times*, October 2, 1949, 3X.

191 **"brick the terrace"**: Letter from Frances Elkins to John W. Turner, April 7, 1950, The Department of Architecture, The Art Institute of Chicago.

AFTERWORD AND ACKNOWLEDGMENTS

Lake Forest, Illinois—on Chicago's North Shore— with its winding country lanes, and riparian and ravine-cut topography, is one of the most beautiful towns in the United States. I was a student at Lake Forest College from 1973 to 1977, and enjoyed a liberal arts education that included courses in accounting, art and architectural history, English, and political science. My major was economics—the closest subject to business—because I was preparing to run a family real estate management business. Economics was not my strength, and although I graduated and went directly into the business, where I happily remain today, I spent most of my time at college studying the history of art and architecture. There couldn't have been anyone better to nurture these interests than Franz Schulze, the art and architectural historian who encouraged his students to visit galleries and museums and led trips to show us Chicago's great architectural landmarks. But Lake Forest offers a treasure trove of classical residential architecture, which became my passion. Originally a summer community for Chicago's first families, Lake Forest was, by the late nineteenth century, the place to build a country house. Between classes, and probably during some, I covered the town, looking at house after house from the road without knowing who had designed them.

Not until my senior year did I hear the name David Adler, when Alison Goss, a classmate and Chicago native, was showing friends the book David Adler by Richard Pratt. I was mesmerized by the pictures of the houses that I loved. It never dawned on me that one architect could have been responsible for such an array of styles. I wanted to know more about Adler and proposed an independent study to Franz. He agreed to be my advisor.

I began by writing to each of the families who owned Adler houses on the North Shore; to some I had introductions from classmates. The families were receptive, and from February through May 1977, I toured and studied seventeen Adler houses. Six remained in original hands: Armour (Lester), Bentley, Blair, Dick, Kuppenheimer and Reed, and in these houses, either the Adler client or a family member met with me.

All were extremely generous with their time, including the new generation of owners. These families had sought out an Adler house and they were as enthusiastic as the original clients about their homes. On spring break, I also visited Castle Hill, Adler's largest undertaking, in Ipswich, Massachusetts (I grew up outside of Boston), owned by The Trustees of Reservations, a Massachusetts land conservation society, and open to the public.

During the last four months of college I made repeat visits to many of the houses. Marjorie Reed (to whom I had been introduced by Lucy Herman, a classmate) allowed me to spend quality time in her mother-in-law's Pennsylvania Dutch stone house, while Jane Kuppenheimer continued our initial conversations and reviewed what I had written about her house. The families always made time for me and allowed me to photograph their houses. My last interview was with William McCormick Blair at Crab Tree Farm, and I rushed the film from this visit through at the lab—the photographs were still damp when I mounted them inside an album, comprising forty-four pages of text and thirty-two pages of photographs, and handed it to Franz.

After graduation, because of Franz's encouragement, I began to seek a publisher for a book or an article on Adler. I wrote dozens of letters and received an equal number of rejections. This, Franz told me, was to be expected, and he even promised to "lay a wreath daily at the shrine of Our Lady of the Dusty Manuscripts." In 1980, Architectural Digest commissioned me to write an article on Frances Elkins (Architectural Digest's first "Historic Interiors" feature, in the July–August 1980 issue), the interiors to be those of the Reed house. Photographs depicting the house in its original state existed because Peter Reed, Mrs. Reed's grandson and a classmate of mine, had recently hired Chicago photographer Luis Medina to document the house before his grandmother died in 1978. Peter generously made these photographs available to me for the book. The assignment (and a second article about Elkins's interiors executed in Adler houses, which appeared in Architectural Digest's January 2000 issue) gave me the opportunity to learn more about

Elkins. The study of Adler always includes Elkins and vice versa, but because my college study was about Adler, I endeavored to learn more about his sister.

After the first article, David Adler did not return to the forefront of my life until 1995, when Arthur Miller, archivist and librarian for special collections at Lake Forest College, asked me if Adler and Elkins had designed the library in Betty and Gardner Brown's house in Lake Forest. Brown was a former Lake Forest College trustee, and he and his wife left the college an important collection of books. When Art went to catalog the collection at the Brown's house, their library's pine paneled walls and coved ceiling covered in silver paper reminded him of Adler and Elkins's work. As it turned out, Adler and Elkins were not the designers, but Art's inquiry prompted me to write a book. Beginning with my October 1995 visit, when I saw the Brown library, I have made numerous trips to Chicago over the course of five years, continuing my research at the Lake Forest Public Library and the Ryerson and Burnham Libraries at The Art Institute of Chicago.

I also built my own Adler-Elkins archive. I purchased Adler's extensive picture postcard collection, which Elkins gave to the Monterey Public Library in California. Coincidentally, the library was deaccessioning the cards, along with Adler's library, on the very day I called to inquire about them. I also commissioned Chicago architectural photographer Jess Smith to take new interior and exterior photographs of the only Adler house then inhabited by its original owner—Jane Dick—thanks to her son, Edison Dick. Eddie also saved for me, after his mother died in 1997, all the correspondence from her files relating to the house's construction, along with the written transcript of an oral family history that his wife Sally and sister Titia Ellis lovingly organized along with Heritage Associates.

I have contacted over one thousand people—present owners of the houses, children, grandchildren, nieces and nephews of the original clients, household staff, archivists, architectural and design historians, and others associated with Adler, his clients, and the great-house era. I have also interviewed some one hundred fifty people in person and made repeated visits to the houses. All these people have not only been extremely hospitable but also generous and trusting with their own archives, allowing me to borrow scrapbooks, letters, photographs and other materials relating to Adler and Elkins.

I am especially indebted to Katherine Boyd and her son David Boyd, Elkins's daughter and grandson. They have shared invaluable archival materials—photographs, original blueprints, Adler's job book, and several hundred pages of cardboard-mounted photographs depicting every building and architectural element that appealed to him, and they arranged for me to meet and talk to almost everyone living who knew Adler and Elkins. They have treated me like family. Many a night the three of us sat around the blazing fireplace in their library, looking at scrapbooks, photographs, and other family memorabilia, followed by a marvelous dinner. On one such evening the Boyds introduced me to Dorothea Walker, the nonagenarian and longtime contributing editor to House and Garden and Vogue, who knew Elkins as well as many of her and Adler's clients. Dorothea taught me much about the world of interior decorating.

A project of this magnitude happens because of the support and encouragement of many people. I am grateful to Hester Griffin and Ruth Winslow of Pebble Beach, for their memories of Adler and Elkins, and to Beagle and Tony Duquette, and Ruth and Hutton Wilkinson (Tony's business partners and friends), who introduced me to several families who shared their own memories of Adler and Elkins with me. Hutton also loaned me priceless stereo realist slides of the Clark house that Tony, who died in 1999, took decades ago.

The families who I interviewed, visited with in their homes, or borrowed archival materials from include: Stewart and Josephine Abercrombie, Ada Addington, Agnes C. Albert, Paul Albert, John Gregg Allerton, Phoebe Andrew, Joan and Henry Arenberg, Aleka Armour, Dan Armour, Jean and Stanton Armour, Lacy Armour, Laurance Armour, Jr., Leola Armour, Pamela Armour, Glenn Atkinson, David Baldwin, Roger Baldwin, Cessna Barrett, Charles Barrett, Billy Bays, Ted Bennett III, Steve Bent, Phoebe Bentley, George Bermingham, Sophia Bischof, Bowen Blair, Edward McCormick Blair, William McCormick Blair, William McCormick Blair, Jr., Barbara Bliss, Ann and Igor Boguslavsky, Nancy Borland, Frances C. Bowers, Joan R. Brewster, Frances L. Brody, Joanne Bross, Mary R. Brown, Neville and John Bryan, James Burlew, Marian Burlew, Arthur Cable, Peter Cable, Dorr Carpenter, Arlene Casati, Fred Castle, Robin Cerny, Countess Camilla Chandon de Briailles, Nina Maria Cole, Ellen R. Conant, Janet and Tom Conomy, Ambrose Cramer III, Nevill Cramer, Peggy and Jack Crowe, Edward Cummings, Jill Dailey, David Dangler, Susan Dart, Alison De Frise, Deming De Grunne, Jane W. Dick, Sally and Edison Dick, Betty Lou and Ben Dillingham, Frances Dillingham, Gaylord Dillingham, Lowell Dillingham, Robert Domergue, Joan and Bob Donner, Brad Dow, Mary Lloyd Estrin, Cantey and Pat Ferchill, Gertrude B. Ffolliott, Jamie and Marshall Field, Merce and Steve Foley, Ines Folger, Harold Foreman, James Friedman, Elizabeth Furness, Millicent Geist, Jack Gillmar, Phoebe Gilpin, Melissa and Greg Glyman, Jean and Steve Goldman, Chissa Gordon, Tina Gorski, Hester and Allen Griffin, Jean Grost, Susan Gutfreund, Bruce Wood Hall, Michael Hall, Stephanie Hall, Corwith Hamill, Ernest Hamill, Laren S. Hasler, Alice and Albert Hayes, Janet S. Henner, Her Grace: The Duchess of Manchester, Barbara and Jim Herst,

Susan C. Herter, Joann Hickey, Elizabeth A. Hollins, Robert Horne, Barbara and John Howell, Mary Hulitar, Harry Hunt, Ginny Hunter, Susan Irvin, Charlie Jacobs, Jeffrey Jacobs, Nancy and Bill Jalonen, Sylvana and Waldemar Jezler, Sidney Johnson, Linde Keiser, Frederick Keith, Jr., Judy and John Keller, Bob Kellogg, Tony Kellogg, Nan S. Kempner, Hi Kyung and Yoonok Kim, Diane King, Dawn and Bill Kirsch, Granger Kenly, Frederick R. Koch, Beverly Kravit, Kathleen and Fred Krehbiel, Posey Krehbiel, Bud Kuppenheimer, Myla and Jarosla Kyncl, Evelyn Lamb, Lewis A. Lapham, Lewis H. Lapham, Roger Lapham, Mary W. Lasker, Gwen Lincoln, Josephine and Thomas Linden, George Livermore, Leola A. and Robert Macdonald, Gigi Mahon, Diane Manno, Ann and Bill Martin, Barbara Maupin, Katherine Mayer, Carol and James Milgram, George Milliken, Henry O. Milliken, Jr., Vicky and Jim Mills, Suzy and John Mitchell, Dorothy Mosiman, Reilly Nail, Antoinette D. Newman, Ben Nields, Sheila Nields, Wirt Norris, Carolyn O'Brien, W. Irving Osborn, Potter Palmer IV, Sally Plante, Colette and Charles Pollock, Abram Poole, Richard Poole, Joseph Pynchon, Diane and Tom Quinn, George Ranney, Helen Reed, Marjorie and John Reed, Peter Reed, John Regas, Barbara Register, Cathy Register, Karen and Peter Register, Kyle Register, Nancy P. Rich, Susan Rider, Diane and Barry Rilliet, Dodie and John Rosekrans, Andrew Rosenfield, John Runnells, Peggy and John Rupp, Patrick Ryan, Tony Ryerson, Barbara Samuels, Ellen and Richard Sandor, Debbie and Mark Saran, Jane Schowalter, Kathy and John Schreiber, Christine Shaw, Julie Simmons, Howard Simpson, Susan and Rob Slayton, Muriel F. Smith, Anna Srnak, Paul Srnak, Paula and Zvonimir Srnak, Peter Stachelberg, Norah and Norman Stone, Patti Strauss, Delores and Herbert Stride, Tom Theobald, Jack Tovin, Elizabeth Van Ella, George Van Hagen, Fred Wacker III, Jana Wacker, Marguerite Walk, Sandy Walker, Murray Washburn, Phyllis Washington, Jane and Morris Weeden, Linda Weller, Lonna Wenner, Bonnie and Donald West, Sidney Whelan, Barbara P. White, Elizabeth D. Wick, Maureen and Tom Wilcox, Joyce Wildman, Ruth Winslow, Munroe Winter, Wallace Winter, Lyle Witte, Arthur Wood, Spencer Wood, William Worrall, Patricia and John Wyle, Sandy and Carl Zapffe, and Carol A. Zsolnay.

I am grateful for the support of my own family: my mother and father, June and Alan Salny, who always saw to it that I had everything I needed to get the job done; my sister Susan, my brother-in-law Dean Trilling, and their two sons, my nephews Scott and Andy; my grandmother Marion Freedman; and my cousins Judy Corsaro, and Linda and Paul Hershenson, and their families. My late grandparents, Rae Salny Brown, Jacob Freedman, and Samuel Salny, and my late aunts, Barbara Hershenson and Edith Winetsky, also inspired me.

At home, I thank my "better-half," Dudley Clendinen, who always took time from his demanding schedule as an author and journalist to guide me, sharing with me his expertise, and longstanding experiences in the publishing world.

Franz Schulze has been a constant inspiration, giving me the confidence early on that my college research was the foundation for a book. He allowed me to see the potential, and I am honored that he wrote the introduction to this book. I also appreciate Arthur Miller's wisdom and guidance. His interest and expertise in Lake Forest's architectural and landscape history has been invaluable throughout this project.

Invaluable editorial guidance and support also came from Mary and Tristan Davies. Angelou Guingon's computer-rendered floor plans of the houses are a perfect accompaniment to the text. At The Art Institute of Chicago, Luigi Mumford, specialist in the department of architecture; Mary Woolever, art and architecture archivist at the Ryerson and Burnham Libraries, and library assistant Susan Perry all have been treasured sources for my research. Jessica Friedman shepherded me with both legal and practical advice. Terry Neff, free-lance editor, was an important sounding board for me as I ventured into the publishing world. Susan Benjamin, partner, Historic Certification Consultants in Chicago, a preservation planning firm, and Dianna Monie, executive director of The David Adler Cultural Center in Libertyville, have been extremely supportive.

Good friends have also been an important component to this project. Among these are Trudy and Mickey Magarill, who "adopted" me into their family and made me feel as if I had lived in Baltimore all my life; Robert Caro, and his late mother Marilyn Caro, and John Winer, who I've known since early childhood; Martin Gould, John Crocker, Faye Florence, Rosemary Cowler, Jack Jarzavek, Janet Ludwig, and Annie Stubbs. Susan Gordon, her siblings, and son Teddy are special friends. I appreciate the support of Jim Abbott, Don Abrams, Jane Baum, Tizzy and Bill Benedict, Wayne Benjamin, Rick Bennett, Paul Bergmann, Bill Bigel, Jeffrey Billhuber, Adam Blumenthal, Joe Boccuzzi, Louis Bofferding, Taylor Branch, Kathy and Gert Brieger, Bill Brockschmidt, Eileen Rhea Brown, Betty Bryant, Tom Bryant, Harold Buchbinder, Jack Butler, Judy and Harold Caro, Barbara Clendinen, Whitney Clendinen, Courtney Coleman, Cynthia Conigliaro, Patrick Cox, David Cyr, Jim Dale, Peggy and Gus Deford, Aida della Longa, Melissa del Vecchio, Susan Hill Dolan, John Dorsey, Richard Dragisic, Jimmy Duke, Larry Dumont, Michael Duncan, Geb Durenberger, Marilyn Elin, Norrie Epstein, Mary Lloyd Estrin, Laney and Bill Feis, Ben Feldman, Lois and Alvan Finn, Betty and Jerry Fischbein, Andrew Fisher, Marian and Hal Flowers, Andy Frake, Betsey Garrett, Charles George, Joan Gers, Alma and Joe

Gildenhorn, Joe Gillach, Hope and J. P. Goldsmith, Ginger and Irv Gomprecht, Ellen and Michael Gordon, Michael Graham, Lois and Leonard Greenebaum, Frank Haas, David Hall, Tom Hall, David Hankey, Ed Hardy, Carol and John Hess, Richard Hilkert, Carla and Alex Katzenberg, Carla Kelly, Barry Kessler, Paul Killmer, Virginia Knowles, Eleanor Kress, Ben Kushner, Mary Lou and Dieter Kutscha, Peter Kutscha, Floyd Landis, Barbara and Ron Lipman, Janet Lips, John Lobe, Ed Lobrano, Nancy and Jim Lucas, Don Ludwig, Fred Lyon, Christy Macy, Jay Marc, Marjorie and Manny Massing, Standish Meacham, Mary Medland, Scott Mehaffey, Jan Miller, Phyllis and John Miller, Roseanne and Bill Milner, Ray Mitzel, Emily and Ashby Moody, Mullane, David Myrick, Adam Nagourney, Nasser Nakib, Carol and Leonard Nectow, Wally Neff, David Netto, Lisa Newmann, Liz O'Brien, Jane and John Payne, Brandt Petrasek, Jill Petschek, Patricia Pierce, Harriet and Philip Plyler, Frank Poppin, Lorrie and Scott Pugatch, Carlos Quezada-Gomez, Jim Rampe, Ben Riddleberger, Linda and Ralph Ringler, Ernest Robbins, Kathy Robbins, Will Rogers, Joe Rosa, Marilyn and Sidney Rosenthal, Vicki and Ed Rubin, Al Ruschmeyer, Sherry and Bob Sanabria, Sandy Sanderson, Gil Schaeffer, Bobby Schrott, Bill Seale, David Seglin, Holly Selby, Julius Shulman, Barry Sloane, Ellen Small, Katherine and Jess Smith, Linell Smith, Chris Spring, Melissa and Brad Spring, Ron Steel, Erica Stein, Renie and Herb Stein, Sharyn Stein, Sheryl Stein, Jane Stubbs, Rose Tarlow, Alex F. Taylor, Lee and Tommy Touchton, John VanderLinden, Robert Wagner, Christopher Walling, Christopher Weeks, Carol Weiss, Jeffry Weisman, Steve Wigler, Christina Wilson, Sally Wimmer, Marilyn and Mike Winer, Don Wrobleski, and Robert Wruble.

I have received endless encouragement from Gary Cohen, Jeff Conti, Robert Ruby, and Lynn and Jeff Sachs and their two daughters, my goddaughter Sara and her sister Rachel. I also thank George Everly for his constant support and guidance.

Among the professionals who share my passion for David Adler's work are Richard Chafee, the Beaux-Arts historian who helped me understand the fundamentals of Adler's education in Paris; Randelle Makinson, architect, architectural historian, and director emeritus of Greene and Greene's Gamble house museum in Pasadena, California, who has been a role model for me; architects Hugh Newell Jacobsen of Washington, D.C., and Stanley Tigerman of Chicago who have great respect for Adler's work; rare book dealer Kinsey Marable and photo archivist Erica Stoller who recognized the need for more published material on Adler; and interior decorator David Anthony Easton of New York—the David Adler of today.

I am also appreciative to the following people and organizations who helped me during my research for this book: Diane Abbatecola, Ron Abrams, Albert Acena, Leanne Alexander, Alan Ambacher, Anita Anderson, Ashley Anderson, James Anderson, Larilyn Andre, Mark Andres, Angela Anthony, *Architectural Digest*, The Architectural History Foundation, Sara Armstrong, Artography Labs, Marian Atcheson, Meg Atwater, Martin Aurand, John Auwater, Fred Ball, Lita Barnes, Wendy Barnes, Thomas Bartlett, Jenny Baumann, Larry Baume, Victor Bausch, David Beatty, Joanne Beck, Colleen Becker, Beth Beretta, Barry Bergdoll, Philip Berger, Kathy Bergkamp, Sue Berry, Charles Beyer, Puja Bhutani, David Bigford, Barry Bing, Angelo Biondi, Joseph Blake, Steve Bloomer, Bobbie Bobila-Peculic, Ralph Bogan, Peggy Booker, Larry Booth, Bill Borzick, Tom Bosley, Justin Bosley, Ruth Boulet, Audrey Bourguet, Jennifer Bowles, Linda Bowles, David Bowman, Laurie Bradt, Florence Brady, Anne Brandt, Jennifer Brathovde, Bob Brick, Sara Briggs, Mosette Broderick, Ruth and Arthur Bromfield, Rebecca Brook, De Soto Brown, Matthew Bruccoli, Will Bruder, Mary Buggy, Ruth Bunting, Shelley Burch, Shirley Burgett, Nathan Burgess, Mark Burnette, Charles Burns, Heather Byer, John Byrne, Dennis Byron, Carroll L. Cabot, Susan Cahill-Aylward, Kathy Cahn, Gwen Cain, Malcolm Cairnes, Chuck Calley, Leslie Calmes, Tony Cardenas, Kathleen Cardoza, Christine Carl, Freya Carlborn, Greg Carlovich, Ellie Carlson, Brian Cary, Helen Casey, Denise Castillo, Cynthia Cathcart, Sarah Cecconi, Dale Cendali, Rose Cervino, Laura Chace, Carol Champ, Essie Chan, Beth Chapman, Brenda Buckley Chavez, Cecelia Chin, Corrine Chun, Maria Churchill, Emily Clark, Jane Clark, Julie Clark, Jim Clayton, Ralph Clayton, Mary Jean Clinton, Mark Coir, Joan Cole, Joyce Connolly, Beth Coogan, Matt Cook, Denise Cordoni, Lynne Cosner, Catherine Cousins, Kathy Cowall, Betty June Cowley, Robert Cozzolino, Ron Crozier, Donald Curl, Mary Daniels, James Danziger, Sharon Darling, Polly Darnell, Lynn Davis, Lydia De Garis, Eleanor De Ropp, Mario De Valmarana, Howard Decker, Mary Decker, Mary Louise Deering, Grace Dehne, George Dekay, Mildred Deriggi, Francois D'Espiny, Willam Dew, Jr., Bill Dicicco, Meissa Dieng, Christine Dimino, Carol Dobberpuhl, Andrew Dobbing, Christa Donnelly, Erica Donnis, Lawrence Donovan, Carol Doty, Lucy Douglas, Eleanor Dowling, Stephen Drew, Richard Du Bordieu, Steven Dudley, Chuck Duffy, Barbara Dunn, Deanne Dupont, Christina Duranczyk, Jeff Durkes, David Dutra, Theresa Dye, Debby Dyer, Marcia Dysart, Bruce Edelman, Diana Edkins, Nancy Effinger, John Eichelberger, Alison Eisendrath, Marsha Eisenstein, Margaret Emmons, Enoch Pratt Free Library, David Esterly, Elmer Eusman, Robert Evans, Charles Fair, Charles Fair, Jr., Denise Farino, Jeanne Farley, Katherine Fausett, Andrea Felder, Lew Fenton, Maureen Ferg, Patty Ferguson, Orin Finkle, Beverly Fish, Eileen

Flanagan, Susan Flanagan, Carol Foley, Christopher Forbes, Jack Forney, Amber Fox, Ron Franklin, Anne Freeman, Stan Friedman, Daryl Funk, Nick Furio, Wayne Furman, Jim Gallagher, Meghan Gallup, Lorraine Ganz, Benjamin Gaylord, John Geary, David Gebhard, Richard Geiger, Heather Geismann, Michael Genet, Connie Geocaris, Pat Gill, Angela Giral, Barbara Glasco, Hixon Glore, Jeff Goldman, Emma and Luis Gonzalez, Sara Goodenough, Ted Goodman, Jean Gordon, Jared Goss, Hilda Gotcher, Kay Grabbe, Bob Graf, Nicholas Graham, Christopher Gray, Ann Gray, Barbara Buchbinder Green, Rhonda Green, Judy Greenberg, Robert Greese, Bruce Gregga, Jan Grenci, Rola Grippo, Mac Griswold, Pat Grodecki, Maxine Groffsky, Toiny Grunsfeld III, Cynthia Guditis, Judy Gummere, Robert Gurbo, Christine Habermaas, Sunny Hadley, Nancy Haines, David A. Hanks, Richard Hanna, Michael Harkins, Kevin Harrington, Robert Harris, Mary Louise Hartmann, Marilyn and Wil Hasbrouck, Anthony Haskins, Natalie Haskins, George Hatch, Betsey Hathaway, Thelma Hawkins, Ed Hayslip, Ann Hazelwood, Paula Healy, Kathy Heffernan, Kurt Helfrich, Chris Henderson, Kate Henningsen, Carla Henry, Carl Hepting, Maria Herold, Arlene Hess, Susan Heyman, Carol Hickman, Bridget Hill, Richard Himmel, Bill Hinchcliff, Leslie Hindman, Alan Hinklin, Alison Hoagland, Elaine Hochman, Gail Hodges, John Holabird, Tom Hollowak, Marion Holmes, Bill Hooper, John Houde, Katina Houvouras, Althea Huber, Carter Hudgins, Ruth Huey, Lyn and Philip Hummer, Neen Hunt, John Hunter, Mildred Hunter, Adam Hydzik, Tom Hyry, Marilyn Ibach, Cindy Infantino, Carolina Irving, C. Oliver Iselin, Mary Jacobs, Elizabeth Jakab, Nancy James, Steven James, Clovia James, Lee Jashelski, Scott Javore, Jeff Joeckel, Drew Johnson, Joe Johnson, Linda Johnson, Nancy Johnson, Ted Johnson, Tom Johnson, Scott Jones, Dorothy Kafka, Judy Kampert, Toshio Kaneko, Daniel Kany, Mike Kapela, Marilyn Kapfer, Diane Kaplan, Gary Kaplan, Bill Katz, Jean Kaufman, Billy Kearns, Ray Kearny, Tomm Keehaus, Jacquie Keep, Tracey Keifer, Greg Keller, William Keller, Maggie Kelly, Norma Kelly, Marge Kemp, Jackie Kervi, Nancy Kester, Margaret Kieckhefer, Kathy Kienholz, Cathy Kilroy, Christy King, James Kinney, Kemper Kirkpatrick, Chris Kitto, Lisa Klitses, Brooke Knapp, Behri Knauth, Elizabeth Knauth, Hedy Korst, Kathy Krajicek, Linda Kreischer, Elinore Krell, Paul Kruty, Katie Kull, Linda and Bill Kull, Jessica Kunin, Myron Kunin, Herman Lackner, Peggy Laemle, Elmer Lagorio, Rik Lain, Bernadette Lamothe, Roberto Landazuri, Guy Lapsley, Ted Larkowski, Dean Larson, Dee Larson, Donna Larson, Theresa Larson, David La Velle, Demaris Lee, Paul Lee, Sandra Leftwich, Margaret Leighton, Judy Levin, Walter Lewis, Laura Linke, Arthur Lipchin, Nancy Lipsky, Tom Lisanti, Carter Lively, Sylvia Loh, Barbara Long, Jerry Long, Marilyn Lortie, Marilyn Love, Talbott Love, Linda Lubovich, Ellen Luchinsky, Robert Lucius, Jordan Luhr, Laura Lyles, Evelyn Lynn, Barbara MacAdam, Robert MacKay, Shirley MacLaughlin, Rita Macayeal, Freddie Mack, Dennis Madden, Athi-Mara Magadi, Kathleen Maich, Virginia Majors, Liz Marcus, Susan Marcus, Anne Marden, Robert Markus, Katie Maroney, Beth Marquardt, Teka Marquardt, Alfredia Marshall, Bill Martin, Linda Martin, Carol Martinez, Rosanna Martinez, Terry Marvel, William Massa, Jr., Christopher Matheson, Cynthia Matthews, Jan Matthews, Martha May, Clemmer Mayhew, Deb McCaffery, Barbara McCandless, Clare McClure, Anne McCormick, Tom McCullough, Megan McFarland, Douglas McGeorge, Dorothy McGhee, Shirley McLaughlin, Bill McGonagle, Joan McGuinn, Linda McKee, Judy McKee, Marilyn MacMahon, Barbara MacMurray, Faun McInnis, Anne McKinley, Lorraine Meade, John Meaney, Linnea Meany, Sarah Medford, Luis Medina, Suzanne Meldman, H. Brett Melendy, Mike Meloni, Linda Mendelson, Connie Menninger, Erin Merriam, Dan Meyer, Murray Michaelson, Alex Michas, Michele Midzola, Linda Miller, Meredith Miller, Betty Mills, Kate Mills, Paul Mills, John Milne, Sarah Mitchell, Pauline Mohr, Tom Montalbano, Alex Montiel, John Moore, Eileen Morgan, Keith Morgan, Laura Morgan, Penny Morrill, Steve Moskow, Archie Motley, Jean Moulin, Tonia Moy, Louise Muir, Jim Muldowney, Lorrie Muldowney, Marla Muse, Jeanette Muser, Paul Myers, Linda Nardi, Judy and Ted Neima, Brett Neiman, Janet Nelson, David Newton, Robert Newton, Kimberly Nicastro, Richard Norton, Caroline Nutley, Cathy Nyhan, Bebe Obermiller, Rodney Obien, Kathleen O'Hara, Troy Oldham, Patrick O'Rourke, Montgomery Orr, Betsey Orvis, Wallace Osterholz, Ayumu Ota, Janet Owen, Mitchell Owens, William Pahlmann, Walter Pancoe, Chris Panos, Margaret Papazian, Rick Pappas, Janet Parks, Tom Parrott, Norton Pearl, Asa Peavy, Enrico Pecori, Ruth Pennkala, Jane Perlman, Dinah Perry, Nancy Perry, Lina Perz, Laurie McGovern Petersen, Carol Peterson, Charles Peterson, Donna Peterson, Ford Petrus, Daria Phair, David Phillips, Sheri Piland, Keith Pizanowski, Charles Platt, Joan Pomeranc, Mary Jane Pool, Charles Porter, Pamela Post, Alan Poulson, Peter Pran, Lias Principe, Ben Primer, Terry Prior, Marie Puckett, Greg Puder, Ralph Pugh, Eva and Craig Quackenbush, Russ Quaide, Lucia Quartararo, Chris Quinn, Jonathan Rachlin, Patrea Rahr-Stern, Jean Rainwater, Catha Grace Rambusch, Monica Randall, Barbara Reagan, Michael Redmon, Gene Regester, Beverly Reibman, John Replinger, Belle Reynolds, Barbara Rhode, Steve Rice, Rev. Amy Richter, Tanya Rieck, Dolly Rietz, Phyllis Rifield, Madeline Robertson, Bill Robinson, Karen Robinson, Rick Robinson, Ian Roche, Janice Rodman, Bonnie Rogers, Susan Rogoski, Leith Rohr, Nancy Romeu, Carol

Rosenberg, Larry Ross, Sarah Rowland, Anthony Rubano, Larry Ruffin, Robert Ruggles, Monica Ruscil, George Russell, Bart Ryckbosch, Winifred Ryhn, S. Salny, Vanessa Samet, Tim Samuelson, Priscilla Sanchez, Andrew Saunders, Nancy Saunders, Anne-Marie Schaefer, Eugene Scheel, Judith Schiff, Doris Schleisner, Lydia Schmalz, Rob Schoberlein, Siegrid Scholze, Mary Schreibstein, Jane Schulak, Ruta Schuller, Joe Schwartz, Paul Schweikher, Jr., Jeannette Scott, Lynn Scott, Mary Sealy, Helen Searing, Pauline Seliga, Mariama Sene, Julia Sernetz, Pierluigi Serraino, Susan Shaner, Woy Shang, Ann Shank, James Shearron, Mary Sheldon, April and James Schink, Brigette Shields, Natalie Shivers, Doug Shouse, Ellen Shubart, Donald Sickler, Kitt Simmons, Alice Sinkevitch, Anna Smith, Sharon Smith, Tracy Smith, Ed Smits, Elaine Soares, The Social Register, Prentice Spelman, Michelle Spencer, Sandy Spikes, Kathy Spray, Sally Squire, Deborah Squires, Chris Steele, Jason Stein, Bob Steinwedel, Bill Stevens, Jim Stewart, Michael Stieber, Michael Stier, Richard Stiles, Sally Stokes, Jessica Stolzberg, Dean Stone, Ben Storck, Mary Ann Stott, Clarice Stromberg, Mary Jean Suopis, Dan Sutherland, Shirley and Michael Svanevik, Elizabeth Swaim, Anne Swallow, Rick Swanson, Ron Swerczek, Rosemary Switzer, Marilyn Symmes, Dorothy Szczepaniak, Henrietta and Raz Tafuro, Joy Tahan, Suzy Taraba, Terry Tatum, Edward Teague, Dan Tenzell, Bill Tepley, Mary Thacher, Evelyn Thomas, Ty Thomas, Colin Thompson, Natalie Thompson, Sharyn Thompson, Jan Toftey, Melissa Tomey, Sally Tomlinson, Jury Torres, Jerry Travis, Carol Traynor, Michael Triff, Miriam Tuba, Sarah Turner, Carole Twombly, Lori Unangst, Rachelle Ungaretti, Barbara Van Lieu, Anne Marie Van Roessell, Vivian Van Wagner, Susan Vicinelli, Elaine Vienneau, Patti Vincent, Deborah Vogel, Barbara Vogt, Kate Wafer, Jeri Wagner, Chad Walsh, Jim Walsh, Bob Warman, Frederick Warren, Tina Wayne, Christine Weideman, Eleanor Weller, Pete Wenner, Millicent West, Carroll W. Westfall, Geoffrey White, Lois White, Ingrid Whitehead, Keshia Whitehead, Abra Wilkin, Nigel Wilkins, David Williams, Sandy Williams, Bonnie Wilson, Gussie Wilson, Mary Wilson, Lynn Winters, Didier Wirth, Casey Witberg, Victoria Wodarcyk, Walter Wojtowicz, Valerie Wolfgran, Cynthia Wollman, Gary Wood, Jane Wood, Lee Woodruff, Diane Woodward, Jenni Woolums, Peter Worden, Tony Wrenn, Margaret Wyatt, Wendy Yaksich, Terrence Young, Eric Zea, Linda Ziemer, and John Ziegweid.

I also thank Nancy Green, my editor at W. W. Norton & Company, who understands my passion for Adler and his houses; Kim Nagy, marketing manager; and Abigail Sturges, designer, whose collaborative input created a book with tremendous aesthetic appeal.

CREDITS

The floorplans are Courtesy of Ryerson and Burnham Libraries, The Art Institute of Chicago and Bowen Blair. Redrawn by Angelou Guingon.

Front Cover: Smithsonian Institution Horticulture, Archives of American Gardens, Garden Club of America Collection

2. Jerome Zerbe, Private Collection
8, left. Princeton University Archives
8, right. Courtesy of Katherine E. Boyd
12, top. Princeton University Archives
12, bottom. Princeton University Archives
14. Courtesy of Stephen M. Salny
15. Courtesy of Stephen M. Salny
16, top. Courtesy of Stephen M. Salny
16, bottom. Courtesy of Stephen M. Salny
17, top. Courtesy of Stephen M. Salny
17, bottom. Courtesy of Stephen M. Salny
18. Courtesy of Stephen M. Salny
19. Courtesy of Katherine and David Boyd
20. Courtesy of David S. Boyd
21. Trowbridge, Courtesy of Chicago Historical Society
22. Ezra Stoller © Esto. All rights reserved
24, top. Brown University Library. Reprinted Courtesy of Architectural Record, a division of The McGraw-Hill Companies.
24, bottom. Courtesy of Jill H. Dailey
25. Courtesy of Chicago Historical Society
26, top. Courtesy of John and Patricia Wyle
26, bottom. Courtesy of John and Patricia Wyle
27, top. Courtesy of John and Patricia Wyle
27, bottom. Courtesy of John and Patricia Wyle
28, top. Ezra Stoller © Esto. All rights reserved
28, bottom. Courtesy of Helicolor France, SA
30. © Musée Rodin, Paris
31. Ezra Stoller © Esto. All rights reserved
32. Ezra Stoller © Esto. All rights reserved
33. Ezra Stoller © Esto. All rights reserved
34–35. Courtesy of Historic Fort Worth, Inc.
34, bottom. Cantey Ferchill, Courtesy of Chissa Gordon
36, top. Kaufman and Fabry, Chicago Architectural Photographing Co., David R. Phillips

36, bottom. Monograph of the Works of Charles A. Platt
37. Hedrich Blessing, Courtesy of Chicago Historical Society
38. Ezra Stoller © Esto. All rights reserved
39, top. Brown University Library. Reprinted Courtesy of Architectural Record, a division of The McGraw-Hill Companies.
39, bottom. Brown University Library. Reprinted Courtesy of Architectural Record, a division of The McGraw-Hill Companies.
40–41. Hedrich Blessing, Courtesy of Chicago Historical Society
42. Avery Architectural and Fine Arts Library, Columbia University in the City of New York
44, top. Bishop Museum
44, bottom. Courtesy of David S. Boyd
46. Edgeworth Photo: Courtesy of Hawaii State Archives
47. Edgeworth Photo: Courtesy of Hawaii State Archives
48–49. Edgeworth Photo: Courtesy of Hawaii State Archives
51, top. Parish Studio, Courtesy of Hawaii State Archives
51, bottom. Bishop Museum
52. Avery Architectural and Fine Arts Library, Columbia University in the City of New York
53. *Country Life*, from General Research Division, The New York Public Library, Astor, Lenox, and Tilden Foundations
54. Avery Architectural and Fine Arts Library, Columbia University in the City of New York
55, top. *Country Life*, Courtesy of Enoch Pratt Free Library, periodicals department
55, bottom. *Country Life*, from General Research Division, The New York Public Library, Astor, Lenox, and Tilden Foundations
56, left. Ezra Stoller © Esto. All rights reserved
56–57. *Chicago Tribune* photo by Tom Leonard, Courtesy of Patti Strauss
59. Trowbridge, Courtesy of Chicago Historical Society
60. *Chicago Tribune* photo by Robert Mackay, Courtesy of Patti Strauss

61. *Chicago Tribune* photo by Robert Mackay, Courtesy of Patti Strauss
62. Mattie Edwards Hewitt, Courtesy of Massachusetts Historical Society
63. Courtesy of Yale University Press
64. Mattie Edwards Hewitt, Courtesy of Massachusetts Historical Society
65. Mattie Edwards Hewitt, Courtesy of Massachusetts Historical Society
66. Mattie Edwards Hewitt, Courtesy of Massachusetts Historical Society
67. Mattie Edwards Hewitt, Courtesy of Massachusetts Historical Society
68, top. Mattie Edwards Hewitt, Courtesy of Massachusetts Historical Society
68, bottom. Mattie Edwards Hewitt, Courtesy of Massachusetts Historical Society
69, top. Mattie Edwards Hewitt, Courtesy of Massachusetts Historical Society
69, bottom. Mattie Edwards Hewitt, Courtesy of Massachusetts Historical Society
70. Mattie Edwards Hewitt, Courtesy of Massachusetts Historical Society
71. Mattie Edwards Hewitt, Courtesy of Massachusetts Historical Society
72–73. Mattie Edwards Hewitt, Courtesy of Massachusetts Historical Society
74, top. Courtesy of Donald West
74, bottom. Courtesy of David S. Boyd
75. Leonard Tregillus, Courtesy of Donald West
77. Ezra Stoller © Esto. All rights reserved
78. Trowbridge, Courtesy of Chicago Historical Society
79, top. Trowbridge, Courtesy of Chicago Historical Society
79, bottom. Leonard Tregillus, Courtesy of Donald West
80–81. Hedrich Blessing, Courtesy of Chicago Historical Society
82. Trowbridge, Courtesy of Chicago Historical Society
83. Hedrich Blessing, Courtesy of Chicago Historical Society
84–85. Hedrich Blessing, Courtesy of Chicago Historical Society
86. Leonard Tregillus, Courtesy of Donald West
87. Trowbridge, Courtesy of Chicago Historical Society
88. Division of Rare and Manuscript Collections, Cornell University Library
89. Hedrich Blessing, Courtesy of Chicago Historical Society
90. Trowbridge, Courtesy of Chicago Historical Society
92, top. Ezra Stoller © Esto. All rights reserved
92, bottom. The Metropolitan Museum of Art, Gift of Mr. and Mrs. Robert W. de Forest, 1910 (10.183)
93. Ezra Stoller © Esto. All rights reserved
94–95. Ezra Stoller © Esto. All rights reserved

96. Division of Rare and Manuscript Collections, Cornell University Library
97. Mary Lloyd Estrin
98. Trowbridge, Courtesy of Chicago Historical Society
100, top. Courtesy of David S. Boyd
100, bottom. Ezra Stoller © Esto. All rights reserved
101. Gottscho-Schleisner Collection of Library of Congress
102. Ezra Stoller © Esto. All rights reserved
103. Gottscho-Schleisner Collection of Library of Congress
104–105. Gottscho-Schleisner Collection of Library of Congress
106. Trowbridge, Courtesy of Chicago Historical Society
107. Ezra Stoller © Esto. All rights reserved
108. Mary Lloyd Estrin
110–111. Ezra Stoller © Esto. All rights reserved
113. Ezra Stoller © Esto. All rights reserved
114, top. Jerome Zerbe, Private Collection
114, bottom. Jerome Zerbe, Private Collection
115. © Fred Lyon, Courtesy of Dorothea Walker
116, top. Jerome Zerbe, Private Collection
116, bottom. Tony Duquette, Courtesy of Hutton Wilkinson
117. © Fred Lyon, Courtesy of Dorothea Walker
118. © Fred Lyon, Courtesy of Agnes C. Albert
119, top. © Fred Lyon, Courtesy of Agnes C. Albert
119, bottom. Jerome Zerbe, Private Collection
120–121. Norton Pearl Photography
122–123. Ezra Stoller © Esto. All rights reserved
125, top. Smithsonian Institution Horticulture, Archives of American Gardens, Garden Club of America Collection
125, bottom. Photo Luis Medina, © Peter S. Reed
126–127. Ezra Stoller © Esto. All rights reserved
128, left. Courtesy of Katherine E. Boyd
128, right. Courtesy of Katherine E. Boyd
129. Courtesy of Stephen M. Salny
130–131. Ezra Stoller © Esto. All rights reserved
132. Photo Luis Medina, © Peter S. Reed
133, top. Photo Luis Medina, © Peter S. Reed
133, bottom. Photo Luis Medina, © Peter S. Reed
134, top. Photo Luis Medina, © Peter S. Reed
134, bottom. Courtesy of David S. Boyd
135. Photo Luis Medina, © Peter S. Reed
136. Photo Luis Medina, © Peter S. Reed
137, top. Photo Luis Medina, © Peter S. Reed
137, bottom. Photo Luis Medina, © Peter S. Reed
138–139. Photo Luis Medina, © Peter S. Reed
140. Photo Luis Medina, © Peter S. Reed
140–141. Photo Luis Medina, © Peter S. Reed
142, top. Photo Luis Medina, © Peter S. Reed
142, bottom. Photo Luis Medina, © Peter S. Reed
143. Photo Luis Medina, © Peter S. Reed
144–145. Smithsonian Institution Horticulture, Archives of American Gardens, Garden Club of America Collection
146. Thorne Donnelley, Courtesy of Robert and Leola A. Macdonald

INDEX

Page numbers in **bold** refer to photographs or illustrations.